Word for Word

D1430742

W. W. Norton & Company, Inc. is also the publisher of *The Norton Anthology of English Literature*, edited by M. H. Abrams, Robert M. Adams, David Daiches, E. Talbot Donaldson, George H. Ford, Samuel Holt Monk, and Hallett Smith; *The American Tradition in Literature*, edited by Sculley Bradley, Richmond Croom Beatty, and E. Hudson Long; *World Masterpieces*, edited by Maynard Mack, Kenneth Douglas, Howard E. Hugo, Bernard M. W. Knox, John C. McGalliard, P. M. Pasinetti, and René Wellek; and *The Norton Reader*, edited by Arthur M. Eastman, Caesar R. Blake, Hubert M. English, Jr., Alan B. Howes, Robert T. Leneghan, Leo F. McNamara, and James Rosier.

Word for Word

THE REWRITING
OF FICTION

Wallace Hildick

W · W · NORTON & COMPANY · INC ·

New York

TO

G. H. BANTOCK

This is an abridged version of Word for Word: A Study of
Authors' Alterations *originally published by Faber and Faber.*

Contents

Acknowledgments

For permission to quote copyright passages from the works named the author is grateful to the following: the Trustees of the Hardy Estate and Macmillan & Co, Ltd for *Tess of the D'Urbervilles* by Thomas Hardy; Messrs William Heinemann Ltd, Laurence Pollinger Ltd and the Estate of the late Mrs Frieda Lawrence for *The White Peacock, Odour of Chrysanthemums* and *The Rainbow* by D. H. Lawrence; John Farquarson Ltd, representing the Henry James Estate, for *The Portrait of a Lady* by Henry James; Edith Sitwell and Macmillan & Co, Ltd for *Alexander Pope* by Edith Sitwell; Oxford University Press Inc (New York) for *Henry James: The Major Phase* by F. O. Matthiessen; Leonard Woolf for the MS of *Mrs Dalloway* by Virginia Woolf; and Messrs Victor Gollancz, Ltd for *Craft and Character in Modern Fiction* by Morton Dauwen Zabel. The author would like to express here also his indebtedness to his publishers for their characteristically unstinted help and encouragement at every stage of the book's progress, and particularly to John Oliver, whose assistance has been invaluable both in early discussions of the general principles and in the numerous matters of detail arising later; to Murray Biggs for his most perceptive and constructive comments, especially when the book was in the critical embryonic stage; to the Keeper of MSS and Egerton Librarian at the British Museum and his staff; to the Librarian and staff of Stevenage Public Library; and to my wife for the great amount of time she has spent in helping to gather and check the material.

6

Introduction

I

PHYSICALLY, an author makes only three kinds of alterations:
he substitutes, he deletes and he inserts. But when the intention
behind each change is taken into account we find a much wider
range of groups and sub-divisions.

One of the largest groups is that consisting of the tidying-
up changes that every author makes: correcting mis-spelt
words and grammatical lapses; refining punctuation; recasting
awkward constructions; removing redundancies, clichés and
unwanted repetitions; and suppressing jingles,[1] unintentional
puns and the sort of *double entendre* that at best could disrupt
the mood of a passage and at worst damage the author's moral
reputation. Then there are the more specialized but still menial
changes that are dictated by the medium a writer happens to be
working in. The poet's minor readjustments to rhythm and
metre, or his attempts to improve his rhymes, would come into
this category. So would the dramatist's changes made in
relation to certain elements of the theatre-situation—the
settling-in of the audience after an interval, say, which might
require a rather longer period of 'freewheeling' on the stage than

---

[1] As, for example, George Eliot had to do when, in *Middlemarch*, she
found she had written: '"What is it, dear?" said Dorothea, with dread
in her head.'

he had originally bargained for in the quiet of his study, or the reaction of the audience to a joke, which might call for some readjustment of the lines that follow—and the numerous changes that have often to be made in relation to the actors' movements: the getting on and off the stage, the need for quick changes of costume and so on. The novelist and short-story writer also have their own special tidying-up chores, particularly where dialogue is concerned, for, apart from the retouching that is often necessary to make a speech more natural or more pertinent (a concern they share with the dramatist), there is the form of retouching that, by setting a speech to carry a larger proportion of the burdens of narration and description, will make it more efficient. And whether the work be in prose or verse, in the form of a novel or play, if it is fiction it will probably require at least a few readjustments to the chronology, sometimes to avoid anachronisms, internal or historical, but more often simply to facilitate and make more plausible encounters between characters. (Timing other than that involved in such mechanical manipulation—perhaps *pacing* would be a better term—is a different, altogether more subtle matter and will be dealt with later.)

So much then for the tidying-up group as such, though we must not of course overlook its shadowy, inverted, Hydelike aspect, composed of what might best be called the roughening-up alterations: the loosening of a speech where this has been made too fluently correct for the character using it; the removal of or insertion of punctuation points in defiance of accepted usage but with a calculated effect (to create an impressionistic mixture of thought and action, perhaps, or to give special emphasis through rhythm, besides the obvious comic and mimic effects of faulty punctuation when using semi-literate narrators); the insertion of a deliberate repetition to give an incantatory effect; the removal of an image that in the context might have been too graceful; the teazling of a too polished, too

8

smoothly flowing passage, to make it rub all the brisker against the reader's consciousness; and the mis-spelling of words not only where the lack of education of a supposed writer calls for this, but where their distortion, or further distortion, can produce the sort of rich ambiguity that Smollett, say, or Dickens or Joyce must often have aimed at when using this device.

Less elementary than the positive tidying-up changes are those made to achieve greater accuracy of expression, or greater clarity of expression, or to strike a better balance between the two (for they sometimes conflict); or to achieve greater force of argument (usually but not always directly dependent on clarity and accuracy); or to stamp a deeper impression on the reader's mind (again usually but not always directly dependent on clarity and accuracy). The power-group, this might be called, where the power to be increased is the power of penetration as well as of projection and persuasion, and perhaps it is the most important of all. In it are found all those strivings after the right word erected by Flaubert into a form of religious devotion and signalled in the manuscripts of some writers by small pillars of deletion and substitution, deletion and substitution—steeples, domes and leaning towers that rise above the lines or totter and sprawl into the margins as first one word, then another, then another, then the original, then yet another, is tried or tried again. Usually the right word so strenuously sought after is factually the most accurate one, but sometimes it can be the most sympathetic or more sympathetic, or most antipathetic or more antipathetic one, as the writer seeks to sway, without jarring, the reader's opinions about a character or a cause. Then there is the type of alteration—found more usually in verse manuscripts—that has to do with the adjustment of sound to sense. In that most excellent treatise on the art of fiction-writing (fiction-writing of any kind in any age)—the preface to his translation of the Iliad—Pope describes this aspect as 'one of the most exquisite beauties of poetry, and attainable by very few ...' and goes on to say: 'I am sensible it is what may sometimes happen by chance, when a writer is warm, and fully possessed of his image: however, it may reasonably be believed they designed this, in whose verse it so manifestly appears in a superior degree to all others.' It is in fact one of the greatest of the several considerable benefits to be had from a study of authors' alterations that such design is seen in process of application, with all conjecture removed, as for instance in Pope's own amendments to his verse in that same work, analysed by Edith Sitwell in the passage quoted below; or in Wordsworth's slight but telling alteration of one word when describing how, as a boy, he felt

> *The Kite high up among the fleecy clouds*
> *Pull at its rein ...*

which became:

> *The paper kite high among fleecy clouds*

—where the sharpening of the visual image is not nearly so important as the fact that now the very pull and swerve is transmitted to the reader by the catch of breath brought about after 'kite' and the smoother glide of 'high among'. Few readers, says Pope, have the ears to be judges of this application of sound to sense, but if anything can help to make the normal ear more sensitive it is surely the study of such corrections.

Attention to images of all kinds is one of the most important elements of the power-group, for the image is, by definition, the basis of imaginative writing, and to sharpen an image, to make it a better instrument of the senses or emotions (a more sensitive receiver as well as a more powerful transmitter), to make it serve more efficiently that 'power of combination—the single vision' that Virginia Woolf regarded as the novelist's most essential gift (and which was indeed one of Henry James's deepest concerns when making his revisions)—to do these things is to help considerably to transform the merely competent into the exceptional. As I have suggested, to increase the power of a passage or a work it is sometimes necessary to make its meaning —its literal, surface meaning—more obscure, to blur its outlines. This is especially the case with allegory, where a too pat set of correspondences can vitiate a work. Nevertheless, though deliberately obscure scenes, constructions and words may be used to achieve this end, and alterations made to mask the too explicit, it is difficult to think of any useful purpose that could be served by dulling images, for it is through them, however strange or distorted they may be, that a reader must feel, even though he may not be immediately aware of just what he is feeling. Wandering about in a fog can be a very stimulating experience and to take us on such an excursion a worthy literary function, but the experience of reading an obscure tale or poem in which the imagery is woolly is about as rewarding as lying in a drunken stupor on a fog-bound park bench and not being able to distinguish the fumes within from the murk without.

Returning to the more usual types of alterations in this group, we find here also those recastings of sentences and scenes that have not been undertaken merely to tidy up. Indeed, as I have already hinted, sometimes the reverse happens, for to strengthen an argument or clarify an issue a series of parentheses, more or less ponderous, may have to be added (legal English is not the way it is because of the cussedness or closed-shop-creating conspiracy of lawyers), while to give greater dramatic or psychological force to a scene in a novel an extra character may have to be introduced and thus knock askew a prettily balanced passage of dialogue (though here there may well follow another round of alterations intended to do no more than tidy up after the first). In any event, dialogue of all kinds usually comes in for a large amount of alteration, both in the first writing and in revision, for apart from aiming at such things as those already indicated—at verisimilitude, differentiation of speech modes from character to character, or consistency in the representation of the speech of each character—an author must often make readjustments the better to record a speaker's reaction to particular circumstances, or to reveal inner stress (sometimes the only way open for a novelist who has denied himself direct access to a character's thoughts), or, by pushing dialogue to its limits, so rearrange it that it reveals true motives and even subconscious urges, as Lawrence does so strikingly (and none the less so by failing or refusing to tidy up subsequently) in the passage quoted on pages 66–69.

Finally in this group I would place the kinds of alterations an author makes when readjusting his timing and those he makes concerning what might be called his placing. By timing[1] here I mean the unfolding of ideas in an essay, or of images in a poem, (which should never be *done* roughly, hastily or haphazardly, even in an angrily polemical essay, even in a turbulent poem)—or, in fiction, of the events to be related: the disclosing of a fact here, the withholding of another there, the introduction of pauses in conversation and distractions and fresh themes where, without them, the plot would roll out with an unnatural, too brisk rapidity. Since this requires a faculty that is developed mainly unconsciously, through experience, it is almost impossible to plan comprehensively for it in cold blood: a passage has usually to be written and read over (or, better still, read out) before any flaws in timing can be perceived—hence the large crop of small but very important readjustments in this category made by most novelists, even those who in other respects might make few changes. By placing I mean the less common readjustments of view-point: the switching at the right time from a position of general omniscience to the mind of a character, or

[1] For a fuller appreciation of the difference between this internal form of timing and chronological timing, one could profitably study the works of Charlotte Brontë, who was so completely mistress of the first and so utterly at sea with the second. In *Jane Eyre*, for instance, the inquisitive postmistress peers at Jane's letter, without talking and without any other distraction, for 'nearly five minutes' before handing it over!

from the mind of one character to that of another, so that a new fact may be disclosed or another kept suppressed; or, where it is artistically necessary to stick to a single point of view throughout, the pulling back to this point of any wandering element. Thus, in a passage in *Middlemarch* describing a meeting between Rosamond Lydgate and Dorothea Casaubon, it was necessary for George Eliot to make a number of alterations so that the reader should sometimes see the two women as an observer who knows rather more about them both than each knows about the other, and sometimes be restricted to experiencing the encounter through the eyes of one or other of them. This the author had to do with the least perceptible of strokes, to avoid an illusion-breaking jerkiness: so, for example, 'Dorothea's face' becomes 'Mrs Casaubon's face' and we are with Rosamond; Rosamond's 'rounded infant-like lips inevitably mild and innocent' becomes 'the rounded infantine mouth and cheek inevitably suggesting mildness and innocence' and, because of that 'suggesting' we are with Dorothea, sharing her doubts and misgivings about the other woman's motives.[1] Wordsworth, using an even more delicate touch, brought about a similar shift when he changed his lines about the moonlit sea:

> *that seem'd*
> *To dwindle, and give up its majesty,*
> *Usurp'd upon as far as sight could reach*

to:

> *that appeared*
> *To dwindle, and give up his majesty,*
> *Usurped upon far as the sight could reach*

—for 'sight' without the definite article strikes a slightly discordant note of generality in a passage describing a deeply moving personal experience, whereas 'the sight' pulls us back

---

[1] The whole of this passage, which includes many more alterations of a similar kind, is carefully analysed by Jerome Beaty in his book *Middlemarch* from Notebook to Novel—University of Illinois Press.

to the immediacy of that particular place at that particular moment of time.

None of these groups is rigidly exclusive, of course, and it is really only a matter of degree to move from what I have called the power group to the group embracing the major structural alterations—the damming and diverting of whole rivers of narrative, the breaking and rebuilding, sometimes in completely different styles, of whole edifices of prose or verse—for where these are made it is always an increase of power that is aimed at. Furthermore, they are so sweeping that they generally make necessary scores of minor alterations of all kinds in every part of a work, just as the tearing down of walls to make larger rooms or a complete new wing will result in cracks in the ceiling and heaps of plaster on the floor of even the remotest attic. So while there is not room in a study of this scope for complete examples of such upheavals—for, say, a reproduction of the dozen or so chapters of the novel George Eliot first had in mind when writing about a town called Middlemarch and of the early chapters of another, to be called *Miss Brooke*, as they were before she decided to fuse the two sets into the beginning of a single, much more satisfying novel, the *Middlemarch* as we now know it—we shall occasionally come across alterations made necessary by repercussion. Where style is the subject of such major alterations, however, as in *Mrs Dalloway*, it is an easier matter to give a sufficiently detailed sample, and this has been done in the passages on pages 116 to 127, where one can almost feel Virginia Woolf's dissatisfaction with conventional narrative methods as she turns from one false start to another with a kind of creative exasperation.

But dissatisfaction, though the commonest, is not the only reason for an author's undertaking such extensive and taxing changes. James Joyce once pointed out that it is in the writing that 'the good things' come, and he might have added that when they do great changes have usually to be made to the original framework to accommodate them.[1] Indeed, he might have gone further still and added that when these good things emerge they do so, for a fiction writer, almost invariably in the shape of character, which, the more skilfully it is evoked, the more vigorously assumes a life of its own. It must happen time and again in every novelist's career that a character digs in its heels and positively refuses to act in a way preordained, and one is tempted to pontificate on this and say that the success of a work depends directly on the maintenance of maximum tension in the resultant tug-of-war. Again there is not scope here to give complete examples of major structural changes brought about in this way, but we shall certainly find a number of scenes changed, more or less drastically, because of the wilfulness or waywardness or reserves of delicacy of such individuals (one hardly dare call them characters) as Tess Durbeyfield and George Pontifex. That this life-assuming activity on the part of characters should be regarded as a form of magic or of divine intervention is a still popular view that some authors seem inclined to encourage, either out of modesty or trade secretiveness, but I suspect that it is principally a matter of psychological insight and good sense—the insight warning the writer that such-and-such a character would not, after all, with a given upbringing, background and set of habits, behave in a way that would illustrate so perfectly the author's views on the Welfare State; and the good sense insisting that he alter either the upbringing etc., or the course of the plot. Many a wise magnanimous author becomes a narrow-minded bigot away from the discipline of his desk—though it is only another narrow-minded bigot who would presume to call his work insincere because of this.

This brings us to the group of changes made for ideological

[1] One thinks of Joyce's *Ulysses*, of course, which was first planned as a short story! In fact when making the statement he was warning a friend not to prepare too detailed a framework.

reasons. Some would regard this as an extra-literary group, though if one declines to recognize any boundary between art and living, of which ideology is so extremely important a part, this description will not be applied. The least literary aspect here, perhaps, is in the sort of change made by an author living under a political or religious dictatorship when he suppresses certain words or passages as being too dangerous to stand. However, even in such a case as that, the suppression often involves a more positive literary action than mere deletion. A skilful determined writer, finding another outlet for his views through parable, for instance, may well increase the literary value of the work and therefore the powerfulness of its effect. This was notably the case in nineteenth-century Russia when, as Professor Janko Lavrin has pointed out, 'the very fact that Russia was devoid of freedom of the Press helped her literature to become a first-rate social force. Since any direct discussion of "dangerous" problems and ideas was muzzled, those problems had to be smuggled into literature in such a way as to escape the vigilance of censors and of the police. A peculiar "Aesop's language" had to be invented for this purpose . . .'[1]

Instances of this are rare in modern English literature, but we do find in some abundance changes made to accommodate an author's own genuine change of views. It is in revision, of course, that such alterations are found most often—revision made after a number of years. Thus, Wordsworth's 1850 version of *The Prelude* shows a considerable number of political, religious and philosophical modifications,[2] as do W. H. Auden's revisions of his own work, so carefully analysed by Joseph Warren Beach in *The Making of the Auden Canon*.[3]

---

[1] *An Introduction to the Russian Novel*. Janko Lavrin.

[2] A detailed survey of these is made in Ernest de Selincourt's introduction to the 1805 text of *The Prelude* (Oxford University Press).

[3] University of Minnesota Press.

Introduction

We are now left with something of a rag-bag of types, some not unimportant for all that they defy firmer classification even in such a rough sorting as the one I have undertaken. One of these is the change dictated by fashion, to be found in revisions made after a great enough number of years, chiefly, as far as I have been able to detect, in the tightening or loosening of punctuation. Another is the sort made when an author feels he has perhaps been echoing too loudly and too frequently the style of a certain model: as Keats did with regard to Milton when he came to incorporate passages of his epic *Hyperion* in the 'Dream' version. Then there is the sort of change made solely on legal grounds, to avoid the possibility of a libel action; and that made for purely mechanical reasons, like the cutting or expanding done to fit a certain space, frequently to be found in the manuscripts and proofs of Dickens (and no doubt in the copy of most journalists). Mention of Dickens also brings to mind the alterations an author makes in deference to what he considers to be the taste of his public. In their book *Dickens at Work*, John Butt and Kathleen Tillotson give a most fascinating account of the author's revisions of his newspaper sketches before presenting them in volume form to a wider, more permanent, 'family' public: cutting out some mild swear-words, toning down slang, introducing circumlocutions where such matters as pregnancy were concerned and, to minimize the risk of 'dating' the pieces, removing the more ephemeral topical references.[1] Hardy also made many changes of a mildly

---

[1] It is interesting to compare Dickens's action here with that of another great writer whose early work consisted of sketches about a city. It took James Joyce fourteen years to get his *Dubliners* published in book form, largely because he refused to do a tiny fraction of the toning down that Dickens had undertaken voluntarily and gladly. Yet one cannot help feeling that each man followed exactly the right course: Dickens needed that great popular audience for his work to flourish and bear the considerable fruit it did, while Joyce needed to preserve his absolute power over his material.

17

bowdlerizing sort in some of the serialized versions of his novels
—notably in *Tess of the D'Urbervilles*, where he gives instructions in the manuscript for alterations made in a certain
colour of ink to be ignored when setting up the volumes. In
some measure connected with this deference to public taste is
that which most writers find it necessary to pay from time to
time to the feelings of individuals. This may also be linked with
the legal aspect, of course, but here I am thinking more about
the sort of delicacy that Samuel Butler showed when dealing
with the character of Aunt Alethea in *The Way of All Flesh*,
based as it was on that of his greatest friend and the first reader
and critic of the manuscript, Miss Savage. Although Butler was
extremely fond of this woman, and although he was free to do
so, he never married her;[1] and if it is remembered that in the
novel he divides his own personality between Overton, the
narrator, and Ernest Pontifex, it is hardly surprising that there
should be such a large crop of alterations in the Aunt Alethea
passages. Indeed, there would seem to have been an almost
hysterical circumspection dictating some of them, and it was
probably this that led him into making a rather obvious
Freudian slip, the correcting of which he had to undertake even
at the expense of detracting from the convincingness of his
characterization at that point.[2] Butler also furnishes a number
of examples of another kind of personal change, much com-
moner, where an author alters a word or recasts a passage or
makes a cut in order to curb his own idiosyncrasies and so
diminish the risk of self-parody. George Eliot does this when-

---

[1] It is interest ng to see how this situation is reflected in the passage
quoted on pp. 75–76 .

[2] See p. 77. It is not until one asks oneself the question, 'Why on earth
should Butler have had this sensitive and immensely tactful woman,
whose generosity is consistently masked by stealth, baldly ask her
nephew whether he would like *her to buy* an organ for him to play on and
this equally sensitive, very polite and unthrusting boy promptly say
yes?' that one looks more closely at the alterations and sees the pitfall.

ever she catches herself using too pontifical a tone or a scientific metaphor that comes too close to being a conceit; while she provides also an example of one of the rarest kinds of alteration: the sort made by a female writer accustomed to using a male pseudonym who, no longer needing to keep up the pretence, catches herself making a statement or allusion to support the myth of her masculinity! But to show the hopelessness of making a survey of such a subject as this exhaustive, or its compartments watertight, or indeed anything but a rough guide to more intensive individual study and speculation, I quote Tolstoy's account of yet another kind of change: 'Usually when I begin a new book I am very pleased with it and work with great interest. But as the book work goes on, I become more and more bored, and often in rewriting it I omit things, substitute others, not because the new idea is better, but because I get tired of the old. Often I strike out what is vivid and replace it by something dull.'[1]

II

To read an author's manuscript can be an enthralling experience, especially if it is written in longhand. We see the places where his pen has scudded along, the dots of the i's and the crosses of the t's trailing behind like smoke from an express train, and we see the places where, in the argot of the profession, he 'bleeds', and words are crossed out heavily, almost it seems with a savage deliberation at times, or intensely thoughtfully, letter by letter, or where scribbled arabesques begin to creep along the borders of the page. Soon we begin to feel that we are actually with him, looking over his shoulder, and this feeling is strengthened when, in a margin, or on a blank sheet, or even, occasionally, in the body of the composition, the

[1] *Talks with Tolstoi*. A. B. Goldenweizer. Hogarth Press. Quoted by Walter Allen in *Writers on Writing*, Phoenix.

writer utters an aside. 'BEDDING' shouts a message in large ornate letters, reminding us as well as Charlotte Brontë that other households than Mr Rochester's have claims on her attention. Again, we find ourselves—if we are not careful—sharing the headache that Samuel Butler must surely have got as he grappled with the calculations made necessary by Ernest Pontifex's inheritance: the long, complicated sums concerning compound interest and capital investment with which the author struggled in many a margin before deciding on the final £15,000. And suddenly to come across such private comments as Blake's 'I say I shant live five years And if I live one it will be a wonder'[1]—or Virginia Woolf's 'a delicious idea comes to me that I will write anything I want to write'—is to be made to feel almost too intrusively close. It is, however, with the alterations that we are principally concerned, for, as even the foregoing general survey will probably have suggested already, it is from a study of these that the greatest benefits are to be gained.

For one thing, such a study can do much to explode and dispel what Joyce referred to as the Burgher Notion—'of the poet Byron in undress pouring out verses just as a city fountain pours out water'[2]—a most persistent and pernicious fallacy responsible not only for disheartening so many beginners but also for allowing them, and the legion of non-starters, to rationalize too readily, with the cry of "Ah well, it just isn't in me!" their lack of patience. Secondly, it can do much to heighten one's appreciation of a particular writer—by showing what he was at pains to avoid as well as what he was aiming at; by revealing how certain characteristic effects had to be consciously developed or certain tendencies consciously suppressed;

---

[1] It was in fact a multiple wonder, the *cri de cœur* having been written in 1793 and Blake surviving until 1827. Above this entry in the *Rossetti MS.* notebook is another of a similar nature, though more succinct. It reads, simply: 'Tuesday Jany 20 1807 between Two and Seven in the Evening—Despair'.

[2] *Stephen Hero.* Jonathan Cape.

and, in short, by demonstrating how skilfully the biographical critic's terrible twins, the Man and his Work, were kept in equilibrium. And thirdly, it can give one a much deeper understanding of the possibilities and uses of language than any set of artificial exercises, because what it involves is, in effect, a series of practical literary experiences of great technical importance shared with the finest practitioners. Each alteration represents a number of problems: the student's as he speculates on why the author made it; the author's in his need to make from a range of alternatives the selection that would best improve his work; and the student's again as he considers whether or not that particular alteration was in fact an improvement. Of course, every printed word represents an author's final choice from a series of alternatives, and ideally it is the critical reader's business to be aware of this all the time. Unfortunately, however, it takes many years for most of us even to become aware of the need for such awareness, and the study of authors' alterations—those scribbled signposts that say 'Here were Dragons, or dead-ends, or avoidable diversions . . .' —prods us into a livelier attention earlier. Furthermore, after being so close to the writer and sharing so vivid an experience of just what he was up against, we shall be less likely to fall into that frame of mind which I can only call critical 'whippersnapperism'—one result of the form of literary exercise which does indeed use extracts from the work of great writers, but only to show how much better other, more favoured, great writers did similar things. It is healthy up to a point, certainly, to demonstrate that even Homer can nod at times, but I leave it for the reader to judge how much healthier it is to demonstrate that Homer can nod quite frequently and as frequently brilliantly correct his slips. To exhibit the nodding only is to give to too many inexperienced and unawakened minds the opportunity to dismiss Homer altogether.

It is with such considerations in mind that I have collected a number of altered passages from manuscripts and printed revisions in the hope that they will prove bases for fruitful speculation, discussion and exercise. In doing so, I have drawn on the work of only those I consider to be amongst the best authors of their kind, and while I have tried to ensure that each extract will yield sufficient material on its own, without close reference to the context, I have not overlooked the great enhancement of value likely to be imparted by a reading or re-reading of the source work and a reconsideration of the author's work as a whole. I have therefore deliberately restricted the field to a manageable number of authors and, wherever possible, drawn each group of samples from a single work. Thus, any one of the George Eliot specimens might serve as a useful fifteen-minute speculative exercise on the skilful manipulation of language for those who have never previously read a page of that author's work; many of the specimens might serve as the subjects of short essays for those who have read only *Middlemarch*; and some could serve as starting points of lengthier enquiries for those who are familiar with the whole Eliot range. But perhaps a few expertly worked examples will give a better idea of this scope.

The first is from Edith Sitwell's book on Alexander Pope,[1] in which, commenting on the lines:

> *The wrath of Peleus' son, the direful spring*
> *Of all the Grecian woes, O goddess, sing!*
> *That wrath which hurl'd to Pluto's gloomy reign*
> *The souls of mighty chiefs untimely slain;*
> *Whose limbs unbury'd on the naked shore*
> *Devouring dogs and hungry vultures tore.*
> *Since great Achilles and Atrides strove,*
> *Such was the sov'reign doom, and such the will of Jove*

[1] *Alexander Pope.* Edith Sitwell. Penguin.

she writes: 'The first few lines of this were changed thus, from the unfinished version, or rough draft:

> *The stern Pelides' rage, O goddess, sing,*
> > *wrath*
> *Of all the woes of Greece the fatal spring,*
> > *Grecian*
> *That strew'd with warriors dead the Phrygian plain,*
> > *heroes*
> *And peopled the dark hell with heroes slain;*
> > *fill'd the shady hell with chiefs untimely.*

'The reason for most of these alterations is obvious. The "i" sound in Pelides, quickly followed by the "a" in rage, unhinge the line by giving too violent a lilting movement to the middle of the line. The word *"direful"* with its huge fiery smoky sound, is obviously better, in its place in the line, than the smaller and rather tiny sound of *"fatal"*, which is not heavy enough. The elided sound in *"warriors"* with its stressed first syllable, and the two following syllables that are so unweighted they can be regarded, less in the nature of one unstressed syllable and one half-stressed syllable, than in the nature of one quarter-stressed and one half-stressed syllable—this gives a ridiculous head-over-heels effect, which is totally unsuitable, and is, above all, unsuitable to the stateliness of the heroic couplet.

'On the other hand, the line

> *And peopled the dark hell with heroes slain*

and still more, the expression *"the shady hell"* are, to my mind, so beautiful that I regret that (had it been possible technically to make use of these), Pope did not decide upon these or one of these, in preference to the line as it stands in the finished version . . .

'. . . The first line of the [fourth] couplet, in the uncorrected version, runs

> *Since first Atrides and Achilles strove.*

The reason for the alteration is obvious. There are too many sibilant sounds in the line; and "*Atrides and Achilles*" gives no sense of heroic strength and combat, but of a weak thing falling, whereas "*Achilles and Atrides strove*", with the long vowels of the two last words, gives just the effect of an heroic combat.'

From these examples it will be seen that even when one's knowledge of Pope and his translation of the Iliad is as extensive as Dame Edith's, it is still possible to make a number of valuable comments on the changes without having to draw on such knowledge. What in fact has been drawn on here, of course, is something altogether richer and rarer: the commentator's own experience as a poet. Nevertheless, these examples may stand as an illustration of the sort of shape one's speculations can take when examining a sample in isolation.

By contrast, we find that it is the direct application of a wide knowledge of an author's whole canon that gives the speculations their point in this passage on Henry James's revision of *The Portrait of a Lady*: 'The growth from ideas to images is what James had been fumbling for in his earlier preoccupation with the picturesque. The word might now embarrass him, but not the secret he had learned through it. He had originally opened the first of the chapters to be laid in Osmond's villa by remarking that "a picturesque little group" was gathered there. What he meant to imply was made much more explicit in the revision: "a small group that might have been described by a painter as composing well."

'That concern with composition grew from the conviction which he voiced in the preface to *Roderick Hudson*, that the novelist's subject, no less than the painter's, consisted ever in "the related state, to each other, of certain figures and things." And characters, he came to believe, could be best put into such relations when they were realized as visually, as lambently, as possible. This belief led him into one of his most recurrent types of revision, into endowing his *dramatis personae* with character-

24

izing images. He had concluded his initial account of Ralph's ill-health by remarking, "The truth was that he had simply accepted the situation." In place of that James was to introduce the poignancy that is Ralph's special note: "His serenity was but the array of wild flowers niched in his ruin." In comparable fashion, James added to his first description of Osmond, with no parallel in the original, an image that embodies the complex nature we are to find in him: "He suggested, fine gold coin as he was, no stamp nor emblem of the common mintage that provides for general circulation; he was the elegant complicated medal struck off for a special occasion."[1]

III

As may have been gathered from the Pope examples, the representation in print of manuscript alterations can get rather involved. Indeed, some commentators have used such elaborate schemes for this purpose, employing what often seems to be the whole typographical range—italics, heavy type, brackets, double brackets, and so on—that the result has often been much more confusing than even a facsimile of difficult handwriting would have been. To make matters worse, most, in their efforts to get as close to a facsimile as possible, have double-spaced certain lines in order to fit between them those insertions a writer makes between single-spaced lines, so giving in print a most unnatural, jerky and (to the reader whose eye will keep passing from line to line in the normal way) irritating effect. However, since physically there are only three kinds of alteration—the deletion, the substitution and the insertion—it has seemed to me that these should be perfectly satisfactorily indicated by using as few, or even fewer, typographical devices —devices which, moreover, unlike italics, brackets, etc., are not in normal currency and are therefore less likely to cause extra

[1] *Henry James. The Major Phase.* F. O. Matthiessen. Oxford.

confusion. Thus, for a deletion I have simply had a line scored through the deleted matter; for an insertion I have underlined the appropriate words; and for an insertion into an insertion, doubly underlined them. Substitutions that are made after the rejected matter, on the same line (running substitutions made in the course of the first writing), need no special mark. When one sees this

> for ~~example~~ instance

it is obvious what has happened. Substitutions written above deletions I have treated as insertions, like this

> for ~~example~~ <u>instance</u>

—and I have done the same in the rare cases where a substituted word has been superimposed on the one rejected, usually adding a footnote to say so.

A very simple case involving these basic devices would be this:

> and then, <u>without ~~the slightest~~ any hesitation</u>, he would go.

Here, 'and then he would go.' is what was first written; 'without the slightest hesitation' was added; and 'any' was substituted for 'the slightest'. The original would therefore be:

But let us consider some actual literary examples, all from the *Middlemarch* manuscript.

1. 'In this latter end of autumn with a sparse remnant of yellow leaves falling slowly athwart the dark evergreens in a stillness without sunshine, the house too ~~seemed in the stage~~ <u>had an air</u> of autumnal ~~decay~~ ~~fading~~ <u>decline</u>, and

Mr Casaubon when he presented himself, ~~did not look~~ had no bloom that could be thrown into relief by that background.

"O dear," ~~thought~~ Celia said to herself, "I am sure Freshitt Hall would have been pleasanter than this." She thought of the white freestone, the pillared portico, and the terrace full of flowers . . .'

While the manuscript arrangement is fairly obvious in a simple passage like this ('had an air' over the deleted 'seemed in the stage', the final choice of 'decline' over the deleted first alternative of 'fading' over the original 'decay', and 'said to herself' squeezed in between and above 'Celia' and ', "I'), it is advisable here, as with a more complicated passage, to write it out in longhand—to reconstitute it, as it were—putting the substitutions in their original positions between the lines. By doing this, one will get a better idea of the order in which the changes were made. Here, for example, the deletion of 'did not look' is clearly a running adjustment made in the act of composition. Perhaps at first (to turn to a consideration of the probable reasons for this and other changes) George Eliot, with her usual clinical scrupulosity, was thinking of giving Casaubon the benefit of the doubt in this case—of saying that 'he did not look as if he had any bloom' etc.—before reminding herself that art can be qualified out of existence and that it is the artist's business to be continually imposing an order on his mass of observations in the interests of the central truth that is to be the theme—selecting, trimming, rearranging and, where necessary, even presenting strong possibilities as facts. A study of her manuscripts suggests that George Eliot was quite often in this predicament, her artistic conscience conflicting with her scientific. We have another example of it in this same passage, where she has substituted 'had an air' for 'seemed in the stage', thereby making the complete statement less clumsy and, while still allowing for reasonable doubts, appreciably more positive. The 'decay'/'fading'/'decline' changes are evidence of the author's desire to attain a different kind of precision, I think, in the choice of a link word that would most suitably describe both house and owner. Again the strengthening of a link—though of another, larger kind—might well have been at the back of the final 'thought' to 'said to herself' change, quite apart from the desire to avoid repetition (the second 'thought' could have been altered to 'pictured' if this had been the only motive), for here it is Celia's utterance that forms the pivot of the contrast between the two households. The fact that it is given in direct speech heightens the dramatic effect considerably, and, in my view, the sharp objectivity of 'said to herself' makes a further contribution to this. The addition of 'free', while offering a technically more precise picture of the stone, does of course further point the contrast. Here, at any rate, the poetic and the scientific were in perfect accord.

2. 'The vicar was a first-rate billiard-player, and though he did not frequent the Green Dragon, ~~he occasionally went to play there~~ there were reports that he had ~~once or twice~~ sometimes been there in the day-time, ~~always winning money~~ and had won money. And as to the chaplaincy he did not pretend that he cared for it, except for the sake of the forty pounds. Lydgate was no puritan, ~~but~~ but he did not care for play, and winning money at it had always seemed a meanness to him; besides he had an ideal of life which made this subservience of conduct to the gaining of small sums thoroughly hateful to him.'

Here, a longhand reconstitution of the sample will reveal more clearly the nature of the two basic sentences and the difference made by the alterations. Thus 'he occasionally went to play there in the day-time, always winning money' will be seen for the stark disruptive hand-out it is, and the improvement made by the oblique 'there were reports' etc. will be more readily appreciated. If we turn to the book for the immediate context we shall also see that the substitution is much more in keeping with the general trend and tone of the passage—a weighing-up by Dr Lydgate of Mr Farebrother's fitness for the hospital chaplaincy—and if we consider the wider context of the complete novel we shall see further the enhancement of value brought about by the way the substitution has been cast: by the striking of the gossipy note in a novel of provincial life, reinforced so beautifully in the change from 'always winning money' to 'and had won money'—the sort of portentous constabular phrase, delivered in a lowered tone and with a meaning look, much favoured by garden-fence know-alls. Again, the secondary change from 'once or twice' to 'sometimes' does more than give greater validity to the statement by making it even less precise: as an item of gossip it becomes slightly more sinister, 'once or twice' having a rather casual dismissive ring about it which tends to conflict with the general portentousness.

The change made to the other sentence is equally striking. Throughout the book, George Eliot seems to have been concerned with lowering the doctor by barely perceptible degrees from the high idealistic pedestal upon which he is first presented, and to demonstrate those slight blemishes, those 'spots of commonness' to which she alludes later. So, in the continuation of the passage, she makes the point that having never known the want of small sums of money it was a comparatively easy matter for him to maintain such an attitude towards petty gambling, and in the alteration she gives this somewhat sardonic reservation a further twist by pointing out that he didn't care for even the innocent play element. (Incidentally, George Eliot left the phrase in the manuscript as 'care for play', without altering it to the 'care to play' of the printed version. In my own view, despite a slight repetitive effect with the phrase 'he cared for it' in the previous sentence, the manuscript version is preferable, not only because it is in closer agreement with the pronoun in the subsequent 'winning money at it', but also because the slightly odd use of the word 'play' as a substantive recalls its more commonly used antonym 'work', too great a preoccupation with which contributes so heavily to Lydgate's troubles.)

3. 'Now that she was alone in her drive, she heard the notes of the man's voice and the accompanying piano which she had not noted much at the time, returning on her inward sense; and[1] she found herself thinking with some wonder that Will Ladislaw was passing his time with Mrs Lydgate in her husband's absence, and then she could not help remembere~~d~~ing that ~~her own past interviews with him~~[2] he had passed some time with her under like circumstances, ~~and that~~ so why should there be any unfitness in the fact?'

This passage, which refers to the thoughts of Dorothea, might profitably be studied in the light of what Henry James had to say of her character: 'To render the expression of a soul requires a cunning hand; but we seem to look straight into the unfathomable eyes of the beautiful spirit of Dorothea Brooke. She exhales a sort of aroma of spiritual sweetness, and we believe in her as in a woman we might providentially meet some fine day when we should find ourselves doubting of the immortality of the soul. By what unerring mechanism this effect is produced—whether by fine strokes or broad ones, by des-

[1] In the MS., thus: 'at the time returning in her inward senses and'—the final polish apparently having been given in proof.

[2] Obviously G.E. checked herself here, crossed out 'her own past interviews with him' and immediately went on with the new construction, so although the words 'he had passed some time with' are written above the deleted words, I have treated it as a running rather than as an inserted substitution.

cription or by narration, we can hardly say; it is certainly the great achievement of the book.'[1]

Here we do in fact see in action the 'unerring mechanism'—though perhaps 'continually self-adjusting mechanism' would be a more apt expression. We see it most clearly in the change from 'she remembered' to 'she could not help remembering'. That Dorothea should have voluntarily entertained doubts about Will's passing his time with Mrs Lydgate and, a married woman herself, have dwelt on her own exchanges with this younger, much more attractive man than her husband, would have seriously impaired the validity of the picture of innocence that George Eliot was anxious to present. But since it was an *intelligent* innocence she wished to depict she couldn't leave Dorothea completely unmoved by this encounter. Certain temptations and misgivings, although vague and unformulated until the final chapters, had to be felt by the character if she were not to be dismissed as an idealistic lay-figure, or as an 'innocent' in the colloquial sense. So those thoughts and memories had to be made to arise despite herself. Now the phrase 'found herself thinking' is a move in this direction but isn't, alone, sufficiently convincing; it smacks rather too strongly of the third-rate thriller writer's piece of broken glass, which the gagged and bound hero *happens* to find at his feet. "*Why* did she find herself thinking these things?" the reader wants to know, being humanly subject to the usual sceptical reaction to reputed great innocence in adult human beings; and George Eliot deftly offers an answer, years before the device was to become a commonplace of fiction, by using the bridge of association—association that takes place at a level of consciousness just low enough to satisfy both Dorothea and the reader, who is now free to speculate on what is taking place at a greater depth without impugning Dorothea's spiritual

[1] *The House of Fiction: Essays on the Novel by Henry James*, ed. Leon Edel. Rupert Hart-Davis.

sweetness. The change from 'her own past interviews with him' to 'he had passed some time with' is less significant—apart from avoiding in mid-stream again a potentially awkward construction, it simply, through repetition ('Will Ladislaw was passing his time with Mrs Lydgate'), has the effect of drawing a closer parallel between the two relationships in Dorothea's mind. On the other hand, the change implied by the deletion of 'and that', from a statement (presumably to the effect: 'and that there had been no unfitness in the fact') to a question ('so why should there be any unfitness in the fact?') is not as slight as it might seem at first glance, for to ask such a question is to point more sharply the dramatic irony of the situation. "Why indeed?" echoes the less innocent, but still quite convinced and sympathetically involved reader.

Interpreting authors' alterations is rather like detective work. Demands are made on one's powers of observation and deduction, on one's ability to spot the slightest of inconsistencies and seek an explanation for it beyond the easy and often erroneous one of accident, and on one's skill at reconstruction ('Now it looks as if he changed this *before* changing that—why? It seemed all right as it stood . . .'). And there is also what might be called the Watson/Holmes aspect. One makes a discovery and evolves a theory which one is then eager to propound. Educationally, this natural eagerness is an excellent spirit to encourage, but in a compiler of text-books it needs carefully restraining, otherwise there will seem to be nothing left for the student to speculate upon. There almost certainly *will* be something left, of course—no one who is at all sensitive to literature would be foolish enough to dogmatize on any but the most elementary grammatical correction—but the seeming will have done its dampening work and Watson yawned or given glassy-eyed assent. So although I have in fact worked on every 'case' in the book, partly to make sure of presenting the most useful and least repetitive of the many I have collected, I have, with something approaching physical anguish, stopped myself from giving any 'solutions' of my own other than those I have offered above as examples, and indulged in nothing more offensive than the giving here and there of a nudge, a slight 'tip-off' where special circumstances seem to have made this necessary.

For a deletion I have simply had a line scored through the deleted matter; for an insertion I have underlined the appropriate words; and for an insertion into an insertion, doubly underlined them. Substitutions that are made after the rejected matter, on the same line (running substitutions made in the course of the first writing), need no special mark. When one sees this

>   for ~~example~~ instance

it is obvious what has happened. Substitutions written above deletions I have treated as insertions, like this

>   for ~~example~~ <u>instance</u>

—and I have done the same in the rare cases where a substituted word has been superimposed on the one rejected, usually adding a footnote to say so.

A very simple case involving these basic devices would be this:

>   and then, <u>without</u> ~~the slightest~~ <u>any</u> hesitation, he would
>   go.

Here, 'and then he would go.' is what was first written; 'without the slightest hesitation' was added; and 'any' was substituted for 'the slightest'. The original would therefore be:

Line Numbers

The line numbers in the quoted passages are given for easier reference and have nothing to do with the original text.

George Eliot

THE *Middlemarch* manuscript is in four volumes (British Museum Additional MSS 34,034–37) and is the holograph copy furnished to the printer by the author. Manuscripts at this stage (the equivalent of the modern final typescript) are usually fair copies, but judging from the number and types of alterations and other evidence, much if not all of this is the original draft. At any rate—and this is what concerns us here—it is quite definitely a *working* draft.

The author's handwriting is fairly small and neat and she wrote on only one side of the paper, no doubt to meet the printer's requirements. Occasionally particularly lengthy insertions were written out on the blank sides, with appropriate instructions regarding their position in the text. But it is her methods of deletion that are more relevant here, I think. Sometimes the line she used was so thick as to completely obliterate the matter underneath; sometimes it was a gentle, ruminative and possibly doubtful ticking-off, letter by letter.

Since she was such a highly intellectual as well as sensitive writer, her manuscript furnishes an unusually wide variety of alterations of a similarly wide range of complexity, and this has enabled me to present the *Middlemarch* specimens roughly in order of difficulty while still preserving the sequence in which they appear in the text. In my introduction to each one, and in various footnotes, I have given rather fuller comments and made rather more suggestions for tackling the material than I shall do later in the book.

I

In most novels, the early pages of the manuscripts are usually heavily amended. The reader's attention has to be caught and held and at the same time certain basic facts about the characters and background must be introduced. Often these facts don't emerge with sufficiently satisfying clarity until the novel is under way, however, and the writer has to go back and make readjustments in the first pages. *Middlemarch* was no exception.

This passage (which appears on the second page of the printed text[1]) forms part of the introduction to the Brooke household—the two sisters and their uncle—with particular reference to Dorothea.

> Her mind was theoretic, and yearned by its nature after some lofty conception of the world which might frankly include the parish of Tipton and her own rule of conduct there; she was enamoured of intensity and greatness, and
> 5 rash in embracing whatever seemed to her to have those aspects; likely to seek martyrdom, to make retractations, and then to incur martyrdom after all in a quarter where she had not sought it. Certainly such elements in the ~~life~~ character of a marriageable girl ~~were likely~~ tended to
> 10 interfere with her lot, and hinder it from being decided according to custom, by good looks, vanity and merely canine affection. With all this she, the elder of the sisters was ~~hardly~~ not yet twenty ~~but nineteen~~,[2] and they had

1 The edition to which I refer throughout this section is that of the Zodiac Press (Chatto & Windus).

2 After deciding on the 'hardly'/'not yet' amendment, G.E. seems to have toyed with the idea of 'but nineteen', writing this under 'twenty' but without crossing that word out.

both been educated since they were about twelve years old
15 and had lost their parents on ~~the most promiscuous plan~~
plans at once narrow and promiscuous, first in an English
and afterwards in a Swiss famili~~esy~~, at Lausanne, their
bachelor uncle and guardian trying in this way to remedy
the disadvantages of their orphaned condition.
20 ~~Only the year before~~ It was hardly a year since they had
come to live at ~~the~~ Tipton Grange with their uncle, a man
~~between fifty and of nearly~~ nearly sixty, of acquiescent
temper, miscellaneous opinions and uncertain vote. He
had travelled in his younger years and was held in this
25 part of the country to have contracted a too rambling habit
of mind. Mr Brooke's conclusions were as difficult to
predict as the weather: it was only safe to say that he
would act with benevolent intentions,[1] and that he would
spend as little money as possible in carrying them out.

II

From another early page (36 in the Zodiac edition), this
passage is part of a conversation between the sisters on the
subject of a neighbour's undeclared but fairly obvious affection
for Dorothea. What difference does the alteration make to
one's assessment of Dorothea's character?

". . . When Tantripp was brushing my hair the other day,
she said that Sir James's man knew from Mrs Cad-
wallader's maid, that Sir James was to marry the eldest
Miss Brooke."
5 "How can you let Tantripp talk such gossip to you,
Celia?" said Dorothea, indignantly, not the less angry
because ~~she had had a stifled presentiment of the fact. the~~

[1] Comma added in printed version.

details asleep in her memory were now awakened to con-
firm the unwelcome revelation. "You must have asked
10 her questions. It is degrading."

III

This passage is drawn from the scene in which Mr Brooke tells
his niece of Mr Casaubon's wish to marry her (p. 40 of the Zodiac
edition). Particular attention should be paid to the alteration
of 'Dorothea's feeling' to 'his niece's mind' and 'his niece' to
'Dorothea'. What is the effect in each case?

". . . However the long and the short of it is, that he has
~~offered to make~~ asked my permission[1] to make you an
offer of marriage—of marriage, you know." said Mr
Brooke with a little[2] nod. I thought it better to tell you,
5 my dear."
No one could have detected any anxiety in Mr Brooke's
manner, but he did really wish to know something of
~~Dorothea's feeling~~ his niece's mind, that, ~~he might~~ if
there were any need for advice, he might give it in time.
10 What feeling he ~~had~~, as a magistrate who had taken in so
many ideas could make room for, was unmixedly kind.
Since ~~his niece~~ Dorothea did not speak immediately, he
repeated, "I thought it better to tell you, my dear."

IV

This very short extract is from Dorothea's letter (p. 45 of
the Zodiac edition—Chapter 5) in reply to Mr Casaubon's dry,

[1] 'asked my permission' is written above the deleted 'offered to make'
but I have classed it as a running substitution rather than as an inserted
revision because the following words, 'to make you an offer', suggest this.
However, there is just a possibility that G.E. did intend at first to have
'. . . he has offered to make to make you an offer of marriage'—Mr
Brooke's speech being as jerky as it is—though there is no trace of a dash
between the first 'make' and 'to'.

[2] In the printed version 'a little' has been changed to 'his explanatory'.

wordy, heavily qualified, guarded and condescending proposal of marriage, which she accepts.

Why did George Eliot make the insertion? Was it merely to add a touch of dramatic irony or to suggest a hardly perceptible feeling of disquiet in Dorothea's mind, which the girl hoped to exorcize by repairing Casaubon's omission for him? Or was it a gentle, half conscious hint to him to be more forthcoming?

> My dear Mr Casaubon,
> I am very grateful to you ~~for~~ <u>for loving me and</u> thinking me worthy to be your wife . . .

V

The following passage refers to Dr Lydgate and the hostility towards him of other medical practitioners in the town (Chapter 45—p. 436 of the Zodiac edition). I give it mainly as an example of George Eliot's dexterity, which enabled her sometimes to spare a word or phrase from deletion in order to use it in an entirely different way from that in the first reading.

> Many thoughts cheered him at that time—and justly. A man conscious of enthusiasm for worthy ~~ends~~ <u>aims</u> is sustained under petty hostilities by the memory <u>of great</u> workers who ~~made such aims possible for him~~ <u>had to fight</u>
> 5   <u>their way</u> not without wounds, and who hover <u>in his mind</u> as patron saints, invisibly helping.

VI

Need George Eliot have deleted as much as she did (which I have put between square brackets for the sake of convenience) in the following passage? It seems a great pity to lose the plant metaphor. (Chapter 46—Zodiac edition, p. 441.)

> Mr Brooke was occasionally irritating, [and the electricity of Will's temper would now and then throw out an

unexpected shock which in its novelty was borne very
well by the good-natured superior. But Mr Brooke was
5 Dorothea's uncle, and her possible presence hung around
him. With pliant youth in our muscles and adoration in
our souls we can adapt ourselves to any corner, like the
darkly warmed plant that bends its stem anyhow if it
can only get its corolla to the light, and] but Will's
10 impatience was relieved by the division of his time
between visits to the Grange and retreats to his Middlemarch lodgings, which gave variety to his life.

VII

This extract comes from a crucial passage in the book (Chapter 48—Zodiac p. 455) where, shortly after Will Ladislaw's
appearance at the Sunday morning church service, Dorothea
feels more acutely than ever before, and possibly more consciously, the dreariness and oppression of her marriage to
Casaubon.

It was another or rather a fuller sort of companionship that
poor Dorothea was hungering for, and that hunger had
grown from the perpetual effort demanded by her
married life. She was always trying to be what her
5 husband wished, and never ~~having the~~ being[1] able to
repose ~~of~~ on his delight in what she was. ~~What~~ The
thing that she ~~cared for~~, liked, ~~what~~ that she spontane-
ously cared for[2] seemed to be always excluded from her
life, for ~~what was~~ if it was only granted and not shared by
10 her husband ~~and not~~ it might as well have been denied.
[3][About Will Ladislaw there had been a difference between

---

[1] 'being' deleted in the printed version.

[2] 'for' changed to 'to have' in the printed version.

[3] The sentence enclosed in square brackets contains a long indeci-
pherable deletion in the MS. For the sake of clarity I have therefore
transcribed the final published version.

them from the first, and it had ended, since Mr Casaubon
had so severely repulsed Dorothea's strong feeling about
his claims on the family property, by her being con-
15   vinced that she was in the right and her husband in the
wrong, but that she was helpless.] This afternoon ~~she had~~
the helplessness was more wretchedly benumbing than
ever: she longed for objects ~~that~~ who could be dear to her,
and to whom she could be dear, She longed for work
20   which would be directly beneficent like the sunshine and
the rain, and now it appeared that she was to live more
and more in a virtual tomb, where there was the apparatus
of a ghastly ~~activity~~[1] labour producing what would never
see the light.

VIII

This extract (Chapter 53—Zodiac p. 500) is from the beginning
of the very dramatic—one might almost say melodramatic—
scene in which the self-righteous Bulstrode is quite unexpectedly
confronted with an associate from his shady past.

One evening, while the sun was still above the horizon and
~~making~~ burning in golden lamps among the great walnut
boughs, Mr Bulstrode was pausing on horseback outside
the front gate ~~in company~~ ~~with~~ waiting for Caleb Garth,
5   who had met him by appointment to give an opinion on a
question of stable drainage, and was now advising the
bailiff in the rick-yard.
    Mr Bulstrode was conscious of being in a good spiritual
frame and more than usually serene, under the influence
10   of his innocent recreation. He was doctrinally convinced
that there was a total absence of ~~demerit~~ merit in himself,

---

[1] Although 'labour' was written above it, 'activity' remained undeleted in the manuscript, as if G.E. was still wondering about making the
change and wished to postpone the final decision as long as possible.

but that doctrinal conviction may be held without pain
when the sense of demerit does not take a distinct shape in
memory and revive the tingling of shame or the pang of
15 remorse. <u>Nay, it may be held with intense satisfaction
when the depth of our sinning is but a measure for the
depth of forgiveness and a clenching proof that we are
peculiar instruments of the divine intention.</u> The memory
has as many moods as the temper, and shifts its scenery
20 like a diorama. At this moment Mr Bulstrode's ~~memory~~
felt as if the ~~evening~~ sunshine were all one with that of
far-off evenings when he was a very young man and used
to go out preaching beyond Highbury. And he would
willingly have had that ~~exercise~~ <u>service</u> of exhortation in
25 prospect now: the texts were there still and[1] his own
facility in expounding them.

IX

The following passage (Chapter 58—Zodiac p. 556) is from
one of the number of scenes in which Rosamond Lydgate
demonstrates how completely impervious she is to her husband's
expressions of displeasure and his pleas for more sensible
behaviour or a more reasonable attitude on her part. On this
occasion he has just asked her, for her own safety, not to go out
riding again. She is arranging her hair and he pauses near her
'as if he awaited some assurance'.

"~~Will~~ I wish <u>you would</u> fasten up my plaits, dear?"
said Rosamond, letting her arms fall with a little sigh.,[2]
<u>so as to make a husband ashamed of standing there like a
brute.</u>
5 ~~The husband~~ <u>Lydgate</u> had often ~~done this~~ <u>fastened the
plaits</u> before, being among the deftest of men with his <u>large</u>

---

[1] Followed by 'so was' in the printed version.
[2] Full stop changed to a comma.

finely formed fingers. He swept up the soft festoons of
plaits and fastened in the tall comb (to such uses do ~~we~~
~~men~~ come!); and what could he do then but kiss the
10 exquisite nape which was shown in all its delicate ——————[1]
curves?

X

Here is a further extract concerning the Lydgates' situation
(Chapter 58—Zodiac p. 560). Lydgate, who realizes that he is
getting too heavily into debt, is considering taking Rosamond
into his confidence and asking her to help him economize. The
deleted passage at the end (which I have placed between square
brackets) was written on the back of the page, with no indication
as to where it was to have been inserted. The most likely place,
however, is after 'each other?'. It is interesting, incidentally, to
compare this suppressed passage with the one of Samuel
Butler's on page 98.

... if any one had suggested a saving on a particular
article—for example, the substitution of cheap fish for
dear—it would have appeared to him simply a pennywise,
mean notion. ~~This may seem remarkable in a man who~~
5 Rosamond, even without such an occasion as Captain
Lydgate's visit was ——————[2] often[3] giving invitations, and
Lydgate, though he often thought the guests tiresome, did
not interfere. This sociability seemed a necessary part of
professional prudence, and the entertainment must be
10 suitable. It is true Lydgate was constantly visiting the
homes of the poor and adjusting his prescriptions of diet to
their small means; but, dear me, has it not by this time
ceased to be remarkable—is it not rather ~~the very thing~~

[1] An indistinguishable word deleted.
[2] Indistinguishable word deleted.
[3] 'fond of' for 'often' in printed version.

what we expect in men that they should have numerous
15 strands of experience lying side by side and never compare them with each other? [I can conceive even that a
man might write touching idylls about the hungry and the
naked, or even be an oratorical regenerator of society,
and yet waste the substance of others on his own riotous
20 living, without being aware that his life was not entirely
~~one in which~~ he offered ~~himself~~ up for his <u>suffering</u> fellows.
He has offered himself up in poetry or prose, and does not
necessarily make the comparison which comes easily to
the bystander.]

XI

This extract (Chapter 58—Zodiac p. 561) is from the same
context as the last.

~~We know that~~ hHe[1] had ~~refused~~[2] scorned even to form
conjectures about Mr Vincy's intentions on money
matters, and nothing but extremity would have induced
him to apply to his father-in-law, even if he had not been
5 made aware in various indirect ways <u>since his marriage</u>
that Mr Vincy's own affairs were not flourishing and that
the expectation of help from him would ~~have made him
angry~~ be resented. Some men easily trust in the readiness
of friends; it had never in the former part of his life occurred
10 to Lydgate that he should need to do so: he had never
thought what ~~it~~ borrowing would be ~~to borrow~~ to <u>him</u>;
but now that the idea had entered his mind, he felt that he
would rather incur any other hardship. In the meantime
he had no money <u>or prospect</u>[3] of money; and his practice
15 was not getting more lucrative.

[1] 'H' superimposed on 'h'.
[2] This word deleted with ticks, letter by letter, as if G.E. was deeply deliberating alternative.
[3] 'prospects' in printed version.

The Middlemarch Manuscript

No wonder that Lydgate had been unable to suppress
all signs of inward trouble during the last few months,
and now that Rosamond was getting into[1] brilliant health,
he ~~began to~~ meditated ~~on~~ taking her entirely into con-
20 fidence on his difficulties. ~~Unpleasant~~ New conversance
with tradesmen's bills ~~in a man who has any reasoning at
command is likely to~~ had forced his reasoning into a new
channel of comparison: he had begun to ~~think about~~
consider from a new point of view what was necessary
25 and unnecessary in goods ~~purchased~~ ordered, and to see
that there must be some change ~~in proportions~~ of habits.

XII

From the same context as the last two extracts, this one opens
with Rosamond's first words on being told about the financial
situation. (Chapter 58—Zodiac p. 566)

"What can *I* do, ~~Tertius~~[2] Tertius?" said Rosamond,
turning her eyes on him again. That little speech of four
words, like so many others in all languages, is capable by
varied vocal inflexions ~~of voices~~ of expressing all states of
5 mind from ~~the~~ helpless dimness to exhaustive argumenta-
tive perception, from the completest self-devoting fellow-
ship to the most neutral aloofness. Rosamond[3] thin
utterance threw into the words "What can *I* do" as much
~~of this last expression~~ neutrality as they could hold. They
10 fell like a mortal chill on Lydgate's roused tenderness. ~~It
was a fatal sign that h~~He did not storm in indignation—
he felt too sad a sinking of the heart.

---

[1] 'regaining' for 'getting into' in printed version.

[2] Another apparently very carefully deliberated deletion, letter by
letter, the final result of which was the reinstatement of the word.
Possibly George Eliot's deliberation here reflected a certain deliberation on the character's part.

[3] 'Rosamond's' in printed version.

45

George Eliot

XIII

Eventually, Lydgate decides that they must sell their house and take a smaller one. Again he tries to make Rosamond see reason; again she refuses. This results in an outburst from Lydgate which, although short, is fiercer than any he has hitherto been provoked into making. The following extract is from the immediate aftermath of this scene. (Chapter 64— Zodiac p. 620)

He went out of the house, but as his blood cooled he felt that the chief result of the discussion was a deposit of dread within him at the idea of opening with his wife in future subjects which might again urge him to violent
5 speech. It was as if a ~~fatal~~ fracture in delicate crystal had begun, and he was afraid of any movement that might make it fatal. His marriage would be a mere piece of bitter irony if they could not go on loving each other[1] ~~He thought that h~~He had long ago made up his mind to
10 what he thought was her ~~negations~~ve character—her want of sensibility which showed itself in disregard both of his ~~minor~~ specific wishes and of his ~~greater~~[2] ~~purposes~~ general aims. The first great disappointment had been borne: the tender devotedness and docile adoration of the ideal
15 wife must be renounced, ~~but~~ and life must be taken up on a lower stage of expectation, as it is by men who have lost their limbs. But the real wife had not only her claims, she had still a hold on his heart and ~~in the moments~~ ~~when she did not exasperate him~~ it was his intense desire
20 that the hold should remain strong. In marriage ~~it is~~ ~~easier to say that~~ the ~~thought~~ certainty, "She will never

---

[1] Here, in the middle of a sentence (a full stop was added after 'other' in proof), there begins a long insertion, written out on the blank left-hand page.

[2] Difficult to distinguish—could have been 'grander'.

love me much," is easier to bear than the fear "I shall love
her no more."[1] ~~tenderly, and his inward effort~~ Hence
after that outburst his inward effort was entirely to excuse
25 her and to blame the hard circumstances which were
partly his fault. He tried that evening by petting her to
heal the wound he had made ~~by petting her~~[2] in the morning, and it was not in Rosamond's nature to be repellent
or sulky; indeed, she ~~was~~ ————[3] ~~pleased with such signs~~
30 welcomed the signs that her husband ~~was fond of her and
that she could control him.~~ loved her and was under control. But this was something quite distinct from ~~her~~
loving *him*.[4]

XIV

Lydgate gives orders to a local auctioneer to begin making
arrangements for the sale of the house, but Rosamond secretly
countermands them, pretending to the auctioneer that her
husband has changed his mind. She also visits the mother of the
only likely buyer—a young man about to be married—and,
by implying that there is no question of the sale of the Lydgate
house, encourages these people to complete the negotiations
for another.

The resultant scene required very careful handling. The false
start deleted by George Eliot has been placed in square brackets
here for the sake of greater clarity. (Chapter 64—Zodiac p. 624)

[1] After the insertion we now resume the original sentence.
[2] The sort of alteration an author usually makes with a hot flush!
[3] Indistinguishable word deleted.
[4] The italicizing of this last word could probably be classed as an
alteration (being indicated by an underline it is impossible to tell for sure
in a manuscript). But originally G.E. would probably intend 'her loving
him' to qualify Rosamond's being 'pleased with such signs'—the natural
accent falling on 'loving'. It was only after she had made the substitution
'loved her and was under control' that she was able to place the stress
(with great dramatic effect) on 'him'.

[~~It was not until~~ lLate that evening Rosamond said to
her husband, "~~The~~ M̄r Ned Pymdale has taken ~~the~~ a[1]
house already."

"How do you know?" said Lydgate, eagerly.

5   "I called on Mrs Pymdale this morning, and she told
me that he had taken the house in St Peter's Place, next
to Mr Hackbutt's."

Poor Lydgat[2] countenance fell, and he looked at the
fire in silence.]

10   That evening Lydgate ~~noticed with~~ was a little comforted by observing that Rosamond was more lively than
she had usually been of late, and <u>even seemed interested</u>
in doing what would please him <u>without being asked.</u>
~~It was not until late~~ He thought, "If she will be happy

15 and I can rub through, what does it all signify? It is only
a narrow swamp that we have to pass in a long journey.
If I can get my mind clear again, I shall do."

~~He felt so hopeful that~~ He was so much cheered <u>that</u>
he began to search for an <u>account of</u> experiments[3] <u>which</u>

20 he had long ago meant to <u>look up,</u> and had neglected out
of ~~lassitude~~ that creeping self-despair which comes in the
train of petty anxieties. He felt again some of the old
delightful absorption in a far-reaching inquiry, while
Rosamond ~~played his favourite adagio music.~~ <u>played the</u>

25 <u>quiet music which was as helpful to his meditation as the</u>
<u>plash of an oar on the evening lake.</u> It was rather late;

---

[1] 'a' first superimposed on 'the' then written separately. A most
interesting change. The use of 'the' did of course give an opportunity for
dramatic irony, but such a slip on Rosamond's part would, on reflection
(almost certainly after 'looking at the fire in silence'), have alerted
Lydgate to her machinations—and this would have affected the plot in a
way G.E. didn't want it to be. On the other hand, to correct the double
slip (character's and author's) and change 'the' to 'a' made nonsense of
Lydgate's eagerness.

[2] sic.

[3] After 'experiments' there is an undeleted full stop in the MS.

~~when~~[1] he had pushed away all the books, and was looking
at the fire <u>with his hands clasped behind his head</u> in forget-
fulness of everything except the construction of a new
30 controlling experiment, when Rosamond, who had left
the piano and was leaning back in her chair <u>watching him,</u>
said,

"Mr Ned Pymdale has taken a house already."

"~~How do you know?" said Lydgate, startled and jarred~~
35 Lydgate startled and jarred, looked ~~up~~[2] in silence for a
moment ~~with the air of~~ <u>like</u> a man who has been disturbed in his sleep. Then ~~with the recovery of~~ <u>flushing</u>
~~a little~~ with an unpleasant consciousness, he asked,

"How do you know?"

XV

As a last resort, Lydgate asks the banker, Bulstrode, for the
loan of a thousand pounds. This is refused with cold piety and
the advice to declare his bankruptcy. Shortly afterwards, however, Raffles, the blackmailing acquaintance from Bulstrode's
past, falls ill at the banker's country retreat and Lydgate is
called in. Bulstrode gives a brief lying account of the nature of
his relationship with the man, and the extract below is from the
subsequent crucial scene. (Chapter 69—Zodiac p. 666)

Lydgate who had the remembrance of his last conversation with Bulstrode strongly upon him, was not
disposed to say an unnecessary word to him, and bowed
slightly in answer to this account, but just before entering
5 the room he turned automatically and said, "What is his
name?"—to ~~have a~~ <u>know</u> names ~~by which to address~~
being as much a part of the medical man's accomplish-
ment as of the practical politician's.

---

[1] Delay-delay-delay is of course the keynote here, as even this small
deletion shows.

[2] 'up' reinstated in the printed version.

"Raffles—~~his name is~~, John Raffles," said Bulstrode,
10 who hoped that whatever became of Raffles, Lydgate
would never know any more of him.

When he had thoroughly examined and considered the
patient, Lydgate ordered that he should go to bed and be
kept there in as complete quiet as possible, and then
15 ~~drew took~~ went with ~~Mr~~ Bulstrode ~~aside to give his
directions outside~~ into another room.

"It is a serious case, I apprehend," said the banker,
before Lydgate began to speak.

"No,[1] —and yes!" said Lydgate, half-dubiously.[2] "It
20 is difficult to decide ~~what~~ as to the possible effect of long-
standing complications; ~~there may~~ but the man had a
robust constitution to begin with. ~~I dare say he has had
attacks of this sort before.~~ I should not expect this[3] to be
fatal.~~T~~, though[4] of course the system is in a ticklish state.
25 He should be well watched and attended to."

"I ~~mu~~[5] will remain here myself," said Bulstrode.
"Mrs Abel and her husband are inexperienced. I can
easily remain here for the night, if you will oblige me by
~~calling on leaving~~ taking a note for Mrs Bulstrode."

30 "I should think that is hardly necessary," said Lydgate.
"He seems ~~quiet~~ tame and terrified enough. He might
become more unmanageable. And[6] there is ~~the bailiff~~ a
man here—is there not? ~~I could give~~"

"I have more than once stayed here a few nights for the

---

[1] Comma deleted by superimposing dash.

[2] Probably it was an oversight of the author's not to delete what her
last alteration had made redundant.

[3] In the printed version, 'attack' is inserted here—made very necessary
by the preceding alteration!

[4] Thus the original full stop was changed to a comma, and 'T' to 't'.

[5] Not very clear. Probably the beginning of 'must', though it could
have been 'am'.

[6] Changed to 'But' in printed version.

35 sake of seclusion," said Bulstrode indifferently. "I am
quite disposed to do so now. Mrs Abel and her husband
can relieve or aid me, if necessary."

"Very well. Then I need give my directions only to
you," said Lydgate, not feeling surprized at a little
40 ~~eccentricity~~[1] peculiarity ~~of inclination~~ in Bulstrode. ~~He
went on to order various kinds of light nourishing food
which were to be offered to the patient, and insisted on his
being kept in bed and in as perfect repose as possible.~~

"You think, then, that the case is hopeful?" said
45 Bulstrode when Lydgate had ended giving his orders.

"Unless there turn out to be further complications
~~which~~ such as I have not at present detected—yes," said
Lydgate. "He may pass on to a worse stage ~~of the disorder~~;
but I should not wonder if he got better in a few days, by
50 adhering to the treatment I have prescribed. There must
be firmness. Remember, If he calls for ~~drinks~~ liquors of
any sort, ~~don't~~ not to give them to him. In my opinion
men in his condition are oftener killed by treatment than
by the disease. Still, new symptoms may arise. I shall
55 come again tomorrow morning."

[1] Deleted letter by letter, with ticks.

D. H. Lawrence

THE three specimens that follow can be said to represent three phases of an author's growth, as reflected by his alterations. The first shows the sort of general tightening and tidying that must be undertaken by the intelligent, sensitive but raw young writer. The second shows the sort of recasting that must often be done by the more experienced but still not fully technically competent writer. And the third gives a glimpse of the sort of improvement—the increase in penetrative power—that can be made by an inspired, experienced and technically accomplished author. That all three were written within five years of one another gives some indication, I think, of the measure of Lawrence's genius.

I

This is a fragment from one of the manuscripts of Lawrence's first novel, *The White Peacock*, a book begun in 1906 while he was a student and completed, after several rewritings, in 1909. The fragment is described by E. W. Tedlock in his bibliography of the Frieda Lawrence collection of manuscripts[1] as represent-

---

[1] *The Frieda Lawrence Collection of D. H. Lawrence Manuscripts: A Descriptive Bibliography*. E. W. Tedlock, Jr. University of New Mexico Press.

ing 'an early version, probably one which dates from the teaching period at Croydon . . . when Lawrence "worked at it fairly steadily in the evenings after school".' It corresponds with a passage in Part II, Chapter II of the published text (pp. 241–242 Heinemann reprint of 1936; p. 210 Penguin edition) which I have reproduced on the page facing the MS. version.

D. H. Lawrence

. . . one had proudly raised his swelling wings and sailed proudly, leisurely after his slim tapering consort. She peeped in corners and under bushes with a feminine curiosity; he remained well out, in full view, and turned
5 his head imperiously as became a reigning monarch. I was much inclined to go down and pelt him with the empty husks of last years flowers, so that I might see him spurt with ready wrath. But I was too indolent, and the orchard was too tempting.

10   There the daffodils were lifting their glorious heads and throwing back their wanton yellow curls to sport with the sun. At the foot of each sloping, grey old tree a family of these healthy, happy flowers stood, some bursten with overfulness of splendour, some raising their heads slightly,
15 modestly showing a sweet countenance, others still hiding their faces, leaning forward from the jaunty cluster of grey green spears; many were just venturing timidly out of their sheaths, peeping about. I felt inclined to hug them, I wanted desperately to know their language per-
20 fectly so that I might talk out my heart to them. They had a rich perfume as of oranges; they laughed to me, and tried to reassure me. So I looked up, feeling my spirit triumph again, and I saw betwixt me and the sky the trees with lifted fingers shaking out their hair to the sun,
25 decking themselves with buds as white and cool as a water-nymphs breasts. Why should I not be glad? For even where the ground was hard by the paths the colts foot discs glowed in merry company . . .

The White Peacock

PUBLISHED TEXT

I watched the swan with his ruffled wings swell onwards; I
watched his slim consort go peeping into corners and under
bushes; I saw him steer clear of the bushes, to keep full in
view, turning his head to me imperiously, till I longed to
5   pelt him with the empty husks of last year's flowers, knap-
weed and scabious. I was too indolent, and I turned
instead to the orchard.

There the daffodils were lifting their heads and throwing back their yellow curls. At the foot of each sloping,
10   grey old tree stood a family of flowers, some bursten with
golden fullness, some lifting their heads slightly, to show a
modest, sweet countenance, others still hiding their faces,
leaning forward pensively from the jaunty grey-green
spears; I wished I had their language, to talk to them
15   distinctly.

Overhead, the trees with lifted fingers shook out their
hair to the sun, decking themselves with buds as white and
cool as a water-nymph's breasts.

I began to be very glad. The colts-foot discs glowed and
20   laughed in a merry company down the path . . .

II

The next passage is from a fragment in the same collection, and is part of an early draft of the story, *Odour of Chrysanthemums*. Tedlock describes it thus: 'The fragment of text in pencil is in Lawrence's characteristic hand. It seems to represent an experimental early version ... Because of the reversal of leaves during writing it seems a separate bit of rewriting, not once a part of a complete text of the story.' The story was completed in 1909 and published in the English Review in 1911. In 1914, after some further revision, it was published in *The Prussian Officer* collection. On the page facing the passage from the fragment I give the corresponding passage from the final published version (p. 198 of *The Tales of D. H. Lawrence*, Heinemann).

MANUSCRIPT VERSION

Then they heard the girl calling shrilly upstairs:

"Mother—who is it?—who is it?—Mother!"

Elizabeth caught herself up, and going towards the stairs, she called:

5   "Go to sleep—it's nothing—go to sleep, and don't be silly"—then she went upstairs:

"What are you calling for? It's only your father, and he won't make any noise. Go to sleep now."

"I thought it was some men come!" wailed the child.

Odour of Chrysanthemums

Then they heard the girl's voice upstairs calling shrilly: "Mother, mother—who is it? Mother, who is it?"

Elizabeth hurried to the foot of the stairs and opened the door:

5   "Go to sleep!" she commanded sharply. "What are you shouting about? Go to sleep at once—there's nothing—"

Then she began to mount the stairs. They could hear her on the boards, and on the plaster floor of the little
10   bedroom. They could hear her distinctly:

"What's the matter now?—what's the matter with you, silly thing?"—her voice was much agitated, with an unreal gentleness.

"I thought it was some men come," said the plaintive
15   voice of the child. "Has he come?"

10   "They only came with your father—and you must go to
sleep, he won't make any noise. He's asleep."

"Is he in bed?"

"Yes. And don't wake him. Go to sleep now."

"What time is it?"—the pitiful thin voice of the half
15   comforted girl, and the plaintive question, were too much
for the men downstairs. One by one they got their caps,
and stepping over the body, they tiptoed out of the house,
hearing the mother answer as they went:

"Ten o'clock!—There, go to sleep now." Her voice too
20   was dreadful in its tenderness. They knew she kissed the
children; and the little ones sank down again straight to
sleep. So was the terror lifted off their hearts.

"Yes, they've brought him. There's nothing to make a fuss about. Go to sleep now, like a good child."

They could hear her voice in the bedroom, they waited whilst she covered the children under the bedclothes.

20   "Is he drunk?" asked the girl, timidly, faintly.

"No! No—he's not! He—he's asleep."

"Is he asleep downstairs?"

"Yes—and don't make a noise."

There was silence for a moment, then the men heard the

25   frightened child again:

"What's that noise?"

"It's nothing, I tell you, what are you bothering for?"

The noise was the grandmother moaning. She was oblivious of everything, sitting on her chair rocking and

30   moaning. The manager put his hand on her arm and bade her "Sh-sh!!"

The old woman opened her eyes and looked at him. She was shocked by this interruption, and seemed to wonder.

"What time is it?"—the plaintive thin voice of the

35   child, sinking back unhappily into sleep, asked this last question.

"Ten o'clock," answered the mother more softly. Then she must have bent down and kissed the children.

Matthews beckoned to the men to come away. They

40   put on their caps and took up the stretcher. Stepping over the body, they tiptoed out of the house. None of them spoke till they were far from the wakeful children.

D. H. Lawrence

III

The third specimen is from a holograph manuscript of *The Rainbow* (published 1915)—a page of which is reproduced in facsimile in the descriptive catalogue of the Lawrence manuscripts compiled by Lawrence Clark Powell.[1] Because of its complexity of alterations, and because it was altered again at a later stage, I give it here in three versions: (a) the draft before alteration; (b) the draft with alterations; (c) the final version, as printed on pp. 94–95 of the Penguin edition.

(a)   As she sat there with her strange dark face turned towards him, her eyes watching him, he began to quiver. She was again the active unknown facing him.

"Why should you think you can find a woman whom
5   you want more than me?" she said.

A turbulence started in his breast.

"I don't think that," he said.

"Why do you?" she repeated. "Why do you want to leave me?"

10   "I s'd think because I'm not satisfied," he said.

"Why aren't you satisfied with me?—I'm not satisfied with you. Paul used to come to me and make me quiver. You only leave me alone, or come to me as you come to tea."

15   "It's no good my coming to you."

"Why?"

"You don't want me."

"You come to me so poorly, as if I were nothing."

"You make me feel as if *I* was nothing," he said.

20   They were silent. She sat watching him. He knew, and his heart trembled, that she thought him again goodly to

[1] *The Manuscripts of D. H. Lawrence: A Descriptive Catalogue*, Lawrence Clark Powell. The Public Library, Los Angeles.

look at, now. He felt his limbs were strong and handsome, he sat in strength.

"You are so foolish," she said softly.

25 The blood beat up his veins like flames, her voice ran into him like fire.

"Come here," she said, unsure.

(b) As she sat ~~there~~ with her strange dark face turned towards him, her eyes watch~~ing~~ed him, inscrutable, casting him up. ~~,h~~He ~~began to quiver~~ He began to boil. She was again the ~~active imminent~~ active unknown facing

5 him. Must he admit her? He resisted involuntarily.

"Why should you ~~think you can~~ want to find a woman ~~whom you want more~~ who is more to you than me?" she said.

~~A~~ The turbulence ~~started~~ raged in his breast.

10 "I don't ~~think that~~," he said.

"Why do you?" she repeated. "Why do you want to ~~leave~~ deny me?"

"~~I s'd think because I'm not satisfied~~," ~~he said~~.

Suddenly, in a flash, he saw she ~~was~~ might be lonely,

15 isolated, unsure. She had seemed to him the utterly certain, satisfied, absolute, excluding him. Could she need anything?

"Why aren't you satisfied with me?[1]—I'm not satisfied with you. Paul used to come to me and ~~make me quiver~~

20 ~~alive to him~~.[2] take me like a man does. You only leave me alone, or come to me ~~as~~[3] ~~you come to tea~~ like your

---

[1] Thus Lawrence leaves unaltered the natural retort to a statement now deleted—to great effect.

[2] Before the final deletion Lawrence altered 'quiver' to 'alive to him'.

[3] 'as' is separately deleted and it is possible that at first Lawrence merely substituted 'like', which is written just above it.

cattle, quickly, to forget me again—so that you can forget me again."

"It's no good my coming to you."

25 "Well what do you want me to do?" said Brangwen.

"Why?" I want you to know there is somebody there besides yourself."

"You don't want me. Well don't I know it?"

"You come to me so poorly, as if I were nothing."
30 as if it were for nothing, for nothing. Paul used to came for something, it *was* something when he came to me—a real man I had."

"You make me feel as if *I* was nothing," he said.

They were silent. She sat watching him. He knew, and
35 his heart trembled, that she thought him again goodly to look at, now. He felt his limbs were strong and could not move, his soul was blind and troubled. She turned to her sewing again. But the sight of her bent before him dogged him and would not let him be. She was a strange, hostile,
40 hounding thing. Yet not quite hostile. As he sat he felt his limbs were strong and handsome, he sat in strength.

"You are so foolish," she said softly.

She was silent for a long time, stitching. He was aware,
45 poignantly, of the round shape of her head, very intimate, compelling. She lifted her head and sighed.

The blood beat up burned in hism veins like flames, her voice ran into him like fire.

"Come here," she said, unsure.

(c)   As she sat with her strange dark face turned towards him, her eyes watched him, inscrutable, casting him up. He began to oppose her. She was again the active unknown facing him. Must he admit her? He resisted involuntarily.

5 'Why should you want to find a woman who is more to you than me?' she said.

The turbulence raged in his breast.

'I don't,' he said.

'Why do you?' she repeated. 'Why do you want to
10 deny me?'

Suddenly, in a flash, he saw she might be lonely, isolated, unsure. She had seemed to him the utterly certain, satisfied, absolute, excluding him. Could she need anything?

15 'Why aren't you satisfied with me?—I'm not satisfied with you. Paul used to come to me and take me like a man does. You only leave me alone or take me like your cattle, quickly, to forget me again—so that you can forget me again.'

20 'What am I to remember about you?' said Brangwen.

'I want you to know there is somebody there besides yourself.'

'Well don't I know it?'

'You come to me as if it was for nothing, as if I was
25 nothing there. When Paul came to me, I *was* something to him—a woman, I was. To you I am nothing—it is like cattle—or nothing—'

'You make me feel as if *I* was nothing,' he said.

They were silent. She sat watching him. He could not
30 move, his soul was seething and chaotic. She turned to her sewing again. But the sight of her bent before him held him and would not let him be. She was a strange, hostile, dominant thing. Yet not quite hostile. As he sat he felt his limbs were strong and hard, he sat in strength.

35 She was silent for a long time, stitching. He was aware, poignantly, of the round shape of her head, very intimate, compelling. She lifted her head and sighed. The blood burned in him, her voice ran to him like fire.

'Come here,' she said, unsure.

Samuel Butler

THE manuscript of *The Way of All Flesh*, from which these specimens have been drawn, is in the British Museum, bound in two volumes (Add. MSS. 39,846–47). Ironically enough—and the circumstance would probably have brought a wry smile to Butler's face—this manuscript, of what is, after all, one of our great seminal novels, is not classified by the Museum authorities as 'select' and can therefore be left at one's desk in the Students' Room, comparatively unguarded and uncherished, while one goes for a coffee, for all the world as if it were merely some collection of early nineteenth-century sermons by a Midland country clergyman of minor importance.

The novel was first published in 1903, a year after the author's death. It had been written between 1873 and 1884, but after marking it 'Revised. Finally corrected and ready for press without being further looked at', Butler put it on one side. According to one critic, his 'failure to publish it in his lifetime is far from meaning that he did not write it with all the seriousness in his power. He wrote it slowly, revised it conscientiously, took to heart Miss Savage's acute criticisms, and kept it in his desk as a kind of investment or insurance against the impermanence he felt his other books might suffer. He seems also to have felt the difficulties under which a book that issued so intimately from his own history labored.'[1] A scrutiny of the manuscript certainly seems to bear this out—the nature of many of the alterations giving clear evidence of the personal difficulties encountered by the author and the extent of the alterations telling of the care he spent on the book. Although written on the same pale blue paper throughout, it is almost as chaotic in appearance as Pope's translation of the Iliad, being not only heavily altered but also liberally cut. By this I mean quite literally cut about with scissors or a sharp knife, presumably in the places where massive alteration threatened to make the manuscript illegible. Sometimes all that remains is a narrow strip; sometimes a fresh piece has been stuck to what is left of a page—in which case the new copy almost invariably bears its own crop of corrections.

Despite the inscription about being ready for the press, the book's first editors had a certain amount of correcting and adjusting to do, mainly of punctuation and minor grammatical points. Occasionally in the printed text one comes across a grammatical error they overlooked, and sometimes changes that are much inferior to the manuscript reading. In my notes on the following extracts I have referred to only the more important of such editorial variants.

I

This extract comes from the first page of the published text of the novel (close on the heels of that splendid opening sentence: 'When I was a small boy at the beginning of the century I remember an old man who wore knee-breeches and worsted stockings, and who used to hobble about the street of our village with the help of a stick') and it is well to bear its position in mind when speculating upon the alterations. That Butler

---

[1] *Craft and Character in Modern Fiction.* Morton Dauwen Zabel. Gollancz.

himself was both a great lover of Handel and a great rider of
hobby-horses are other considerations worth taking into
account, not only in the present passage but in other extracts
from this most personal of novels.

Mr Pontifex ~~had developed in ways that were unusual
in those days for one in his position at the begin~~ .His
~~trade was that of a~~ was a carpenter[1] by trade;[2] he was
also at one time parish clerk; when I remember him,
5   however, he had so far risen in life as to be ~~beyond the
necessity of working~~ no long[3] compelled to work with his
own hands. In his earlier days he had taught himself to
draw. I do not say he drew well, but it was surprising he
should draw as well as he did. My father, who ~~became
10   rector~~ took the living of Paleham about the year 1797,
became possessed of a good many of old Mr Pontifex's
drawings which were always of local subjects, and ~~had the
merit of a direct simple minded painstakingness which
made them like the drawings of some early Flemish painter
15   so painstaking~~ so unaffectedly painstaking that they ~~were
more like~~ might have passed for the work of ~~an~~ some
~~early master, but ex~~ good early master; I remember
them as hanging up framed and glazed in the study at the
Rectory, and tinted, as all else in the room was tinted,
20   with the green reflected from the fringe of ivy leaves that
~~hung~~ grew around the windows. I wonder how they will

[1] Comma deleted after 'carpenter'.

[2] A good example for practising one's skill at reconstruction. Butler's
first attempt was 'Mr Pontifex had developed in ways that were unusual
for one in his position at the begin . . .' where he presumably intended 'at
the beginning of the century'. This last was discarded for 'in those days'.
'that of a carpenter' seems to refer to 'position' and 'a' was probably
deleted first. The insertions, 'His trade was' and 'was a' and 'by trade'
were all in a different coloured ink and presumably made at a later date.

[3] Sic. This insertion was also made later.

66

actually cease and come to an end as drawings, and into[1]
what new phases of being they will then enter.

Not content with being an artist, Mr Pontifex must
25 needs also be a musician. He built the organ in the
church with his own hands, and ~~he~~ made a smaller one
which he kept in his own house. He could play much as
he could draw; not ~~indeed well~~ very well according to
professional standards, but much better than could have
30 been expected. ~~He worshipped Handel whom as a young
man he had seen when he was on his way to Dublin, and
for whom, if I mistake not he had executed some small
errand or commission~~; this fact had perhaps intensified
the old man's admiration, but at any rate he was as certain
35 ~~that Handel was the greatest of all musicians, past,
present and to come as that Shakespeare was the prince
of all possible writers.~~ I myself ~~took to Handel at a very~~
showed a taste for music at an early age, and old Mr
Pontifex ~~soon found it out and~~ on finding it out, as he
40 soon did, became partial to me ~~at once, for there is nothing
that goes so straight home to the heart of a good Handelian,
as to observe an instinctive love for Handel's music in a
child.~~ in consequence.

It may be thought that with so many irons in the fire he
45 could hardly be a very thriving man, but this was not the
case. His father had been a day labourer, and he himself
had begun life with no other capital than his good sense
and good constitution; now, however, there was a goodly
show of timber about his yard, and a look of solid comfort
50 over his whole establishment.[2]

~~Mrs Pontifex made an admirable wife as far as thrift~~

---

[1] Quite plainly 'into' in the MS., but given as 'in' in the published text.
[2] At this point, in the space before what was to have been a new
paragraph, the instruction 'run on' has been written: i.e., continue the
same paragraph.

~~and neatness~~ ~~were~~ ~~concerned~~; ̶tTowards the close of the
last century[1] and not ~~so~~ ~~very~~ long before my father came
to Paleham, ~~her~~ ~~husband~~ he[2] had taken a farm of about
55 ninety acres, thus making a considerable rise in life.

II

From the end of Chapter 1 (Collins New Classics p. 21). Here
the narrator has been recalling an argument he had as a young
man with his father, about old Pontifex. It has ended with his
father's words: "". . . his grammar may have been imperfect,
but . . . I say again, Edward, that old Pontifex was not only an
able man, but one of the very ablest men I ever knew.""
The major deletion has been put in square brackets, its
interior alterations being shown in the usual way.

Against this there was no more to be said, and my
sisters eyed me to silence. Somehow or other my sisters
always did eye me to silence when I differed from my
father. ~~In this case however~~
5   [I have no doubt my father was right, for I have never
been a convert to that modern doctrine which holds that a
man's life and his work may be two distinct things of
which the one may be ~~very~~ good and the other bad.
I hold rather with the old view, that ~~the~~ work and ~~the~~
10 man are as ~~the~~ fruit and ~~the~~ tree, and that a corrupt tree
cannot bring forth good fruit nor a good tree evil fruit. If
the fruit is ~~good~~ known, and good beware how you say the
life was evil; if the life ~~wa~~ is known and evil beware how
you say the fruit is good. If we want to know what a man
15 was we had better look at his work as a general rule than

[1] Changed in the published text to 'eighteenth century'.

[2] Note how, by deferring Mrs Pontifex's entry, Butler has created a
slight ambiguity here. To see just how long Mrs Pontifex's entry was
deferred, and how her full introduction was eventually made (she had
already been briefly mentioned on the first page), and whether this
was an improvement on the original intention, see the book.

at what is said about his life. The actual facts concerning
the work are more certain; there it is; in it we have the
man's soul written out with his own hand; moreover it
remains more still, so that we can think about it at
20 leisure, and more isolated from surroundings of which we
know nothing and from the lies of rivals. The old saying
of Buffon's that the style is the man himself is as near the
truth as we can get—but then most men mistake grammar
for style, as they mistake correct spelling for words
25 schooling for education.]

"Talk of his successful son," snorted my father, whom I
had fairly roused, "he is not fit to black his father's boots.
He has his thousands of pounds a year, while his father had
perhaps three thousand shillings a year towards the end of
30 his life; he *is* a successful man; but his father, hobbling
about Paleham Street in his grey worsted stocking, broad
brimmed hat and brown swallow tailed coat was worth a
hundred of George Pontifexes, for all his carriages and
horses and the airs he gives himself.[1]

35 "But yet," he added, "George Pontifex is no fool
either." And this brings us to the second generation of the
Pontifex family with whom we need concern ourselves.

III

In considering the main alteration in this passage (from
Chapter 3, Collins New Classics p. 25), it is necessary to know the
book's plot. It is in fact one of the most common—and most
important—types of alterations made by novelists.

---

[1] Here the speech was originally closed. The quotation marks were
deleted, however, and the final short paragraph added—a significant
alteration, coming as it does at the end of the first chapter. Whether it was
added immediately or later, in revision, is uncertain, since presumably
the last inch or so of the MS. page would have been left blank anyway,
and the new chapter started on a fresh sheet.

By us, at the Rectory, there was no time so much looked
forward to as the annual visit of the little Pontifexes to
Paleham. We came in for some of the prevailing licence;
we went to tea with Mrs Pontifex to meet her grand-
5 children, and then our young friends were asked to the
rectory to have tea with us, and we had what we considered great times. I fell desperately in love with
~~little~~ Alethea, indeed we all fell in love with each other,
~~higgledy piggledy and~~ plurality and exchange whether
10 of wives or husbands ~~was~~ being openly and unblushingly
advocated in the very presence of our nurses; ~~vastly very
vastly merry were we, .~~ We were very merry, but it is
so long ago that I have forgotten almost all[1] save that we
were[2] ~~vastly~~ vastly very[3] merry.[4] ~~but~~ almost the only
15 thing that remains with me as a permanent impression
was the fact that Theobald one day beat his nurse and
teased her, and when she said she should go away cried
out—"You shan't go away— ~~you shan't go away~~. I'll keep
you on purpose to torment you."

IV

From Chapter 6 (Collins New Classics p. 39), this passage is
about George Pontifex's (and Samuel Butler's) views on
education. Again it is necessary to have a knowledge of the plot
when considering the main alteration.

He pitied himself for the expensive education which he
was giving his children; he did not see that the education

---

[1] In the published text changed to 'nearly everything'.

[2] In the published text 'were' italicized.

[3] Here Butler first wrote 'vastly', deleted it, then made a 'stet' note
for it to stand, which he failed to cancel when inserting 'very'.

[4] First a full stop, then a comma added to make it a semi-colon, then
the comma deleted to make it a full stop again.

cost the children far more than it cost him, inasmuch as
it cost them the power of earning their living easily rather
5   than helped them towards it, and ensured their being
~~dependent upon~~ at the mercy of their father for years
after they ~~have~~ had come to an age when they should be
independent. ~~He had no conception of this~~: ~~all he *saw* was~~
~~that he was spending much more~~ A public school education
10 cuts off a boy's retreat; he can no longer become a labourer
or a mechanic, and these are the only people whose tenure
of independence is not precarious ~~unless of~~ with the
exception of course of those who are born inheritors of
money, or who are placed young in some safe and deep
15 groove. Mr Pontifex saw nothing of this; all he saw was
that he was spending much more money upon his children
than the law would have compelled him to do, and what
more could you have?

V

I give here the manuscript version of the famous Chapter 17
almost in its entirety. It contains a wide range of types of
alterations, including the important one—perhaps especially
important in comic writing—of dramatic timing. Note also the
changes that alter tone, and their effect.

~~Towards the close~~ At the beginning of the ~~fourth~~ fifth
year of her married life Mrs Theobald[1] was safely delivered
of a boy. This was on the sixth of September 1835.
Word was immediately sent to old Mr Pontifex,[2] who
5   received the news with real pleasure. His son John's wife
had borne daughters only, and ~~the old gentleman was~~
~~getting uneasy~~ he was seriously uneasy lest there should

[1] Changed to 'Christina' by the editors of the published text.
[2] I.e., George Pontifex.

be a failure in the male line of his descendants. ~~Now,~~
~~therefore, that~~ tThe good news ~~came it~~ therefore was
10 doubly welcome and caused as much delight at Elmhurst
as dismay in Woburn Square,[1] where the John Pontifexes
were then living.

Here, indeed, this freak of fortune was felt to be all the
more cruel on account of the impossibility of resenting it
15 openly; but ~~this was nothing to the delighted grandfather.~~
~~He~~ the delighted grandfather cared nothing ~~about this~~;
for what the John Pontifexes might feel or not feel; he
had wanted a ~~male grandchild~~ grandson and he had
got a ~~male grandchild~~ grandson; ~~that~~ this should be
20 enough for everybody; and now that Mrs Theobald had
taken to good ways she might bring him more grandsons,
which ~~might be desirable~~ would be desirable—for he
should not feel safe with ~~less~~ fewer than three.

He rang the bell for the butler.
25 "Gelstrap" he said solemnly "I want to go down into the
cellar."

Then Gelstrap preceded him with a candle, and he
went into the inner vault ~~of vaults~~ where he kept his
choicest wines.

He passed many bins; There was Port 1803; Imperial
30 Tokay 1792, claret 1800, sherry 1812;[2] these and many
others were passed ~~with an affectionate glan~~[3] but it was
not for them that the head of the Pontifex family had
gone down into his inner cellar. A bin which ~~by until the~~
~~feeble light of the candle had appeared empty was at last~~
35 ~~reached~~ had appeared empty until the full light of the

[1] Probably Butler had been thinking of writing 'as in Woburn Square it
caused dismay'. The published text has 'at' for 'in'.

[2] The published text has the dates and names reversed, perhaps in-
sensitively, for Butler's is surely the order in which the smug old man
would think of them as he caught sight of each bin.

[3] This could have been 'glare' and not the beginning of 'glance'.

candle had been brought to bear upon it was now found
to contain a single ~~small~~ pint bottle. This was the object
of Mr Pontifex's search.

Gelstrap had often pondered over this bottle. It had
40 been placed there by Mr Pontifex himself about a dozen
years previously, on his return from a visit to his friend
the celebrated traveller Dr Jones—but there was no
tablet above the bin which might give a clue to the
nature of its contents. On more than one occasion when
45 his master had gone out and left his keys accidentally
behind him, as he sometimes did, Gelstrap had submitted
~~this bottle~~ it to all the tests ~~which his limited resources~~
~~would allow~~; he could venture upon, but it was so carefully
sealed that wisdom ~~at that entrance which would have~~
50 ~~been most pleasing to him remained quite shut out, and~~[1]
remained quite shut out from that entrance at which he
would have welcomed her most gladly, ~~and he was had~~
~~been obliged therefore to to content himself with the~~
~~negative conclusion that there was nothing to be made out~~
55 ~~concerning the mysterious bottle~~ it. and indeed from
all other entrances, for he could make out nothing at all.

And now the mystery was to be solved. But Alas! it
seemed as though the last chance of securing even a sip of
the contents was to be removed for ever, for Mr Pontifex
60 took the bottle into his own hands and held it up to the
light after carefully examining the seal. He ~~then~~ smiled
~~with evident satisfaction, and retreated~~ began to return[2]

---

[1] A close study of the MS. suggests that Butler stopped here and made
his deletion from 'at that . . .' The substitution was written above the
deletion, B. then continuing normally from 'obliged'. The insertion
'therefore to' and the substitution of 'it' for 'the mysterious bottle'
were obviously made before the whole of this last part of the sentence
was deleted and the 'and indeed . . . at all' substitution made.

[2] 'began to return' substituted for 'retreated' before longer deletion
made.

~~slowly~~ ~~with~~ ~~his~~ ~~prize.~~ and left the bin with the bottle in
his hands.

65   Then came a ~~terrible~~ catastrophe. He stumbled over
an empty hamper; there was a sound of a fall—a smash of
broken glass, and in an instant the cellar floor was
covered with the liquid that had been preserved so
carefully for so many years.

70   With his usual presence of mind Mr Pontifex gasped
out a ~~week's~~ month's warning to Gelstrap. Then he got
up, ~~and stamped~~ and stamped, ~~and~~ ~~and I am ashamed to~~
~~say, he~~ ~~swore~~ ~~great~~ ~~oaths~~ ~~more~~ ~~than~~ ~~once~~ ~~in~~ ~~the~~ ~~most~~
~~offensive~~ ~~manner~~ ~~conceivable~~ just ~~like~~ as ~~Christina~~ ~~had~~
75   ~~done~~ Theobald had done when Christina had wanted not
to order his dinner. ~~As seen in the gloom of the cellar~~[1]

"It's water from the JORDAN," he exclaimed ~~wildly~~
furiously "which I have been saving for the baptism of
my eldest grandson "D—n[2] you Gelstrap, how dared
80   ~~you with your~~ ~~infernal~~ ~~carelessness~~ ~~to~~ ~~leave~~ ~~that~~ ~~d—d~~
~~hamper~~ ~~in~~ ~~the~~ ~~cellar?~~ you be so infernally careless as to
leave that hamper littering about ~~d~~ the cellar?[3]

I wonder the waters[4] of the sacred stream did not
stand upright as an heap ~~and~~ ~~rebuke~~ upon the cellar
85   floor, and rebuke ~~his~~ ~~impious~~ ~~such~~ ~~horrid~~ ~~language~~ ~~such~~
~~language~~ him. Gelstrap told the other servants after-

---

[1] Here the first change was the deletion of 'and stamped', after which
Butler proceeded with the cursing description. This was later deleted
and, reverting to the stamping, Butler reinstated 'and stamped' and
continued with the Theobald/Christina echo. After 'cellar' the page
has been cut, thereby removing completely further deleted material.

[2] Written thus, with quotation marks (the original closing marks after
'grandson' perhaps, this direct sample of Mr Pontifex's cursing being
given as an afterthought). The published text gives 'Damn' in full.

[3] Quotation marks not closed. Butler's punctuation seems to have
been sacrificed to his zest in the whole of this passage.

[4] 'water' in published text—another insensitive change, I feel.

wards that his master's ~~words~~ language had made his
back bone curdle.

90 "~~Water,~~" ~~said~~ ~~Gelstrap~~ ~~to~~ ~~himself—and~~ ~~his~~ ~~swift~~ ~~soul~~ ~~urged~~ ~~him~~ ~~he~~ ~~flew~~ ~~to~~ ~~his~~ ~~pantry.~~ ~~Before~~ The moment,
however that he heard the word "water", he ~~showed~~ ~~great~~ ~~presence~~ ~~of~~ ~~mind.~~ ~~He~~ saw his way again, and flew
to the pantry; ~~and~~ ~~b.~~Before[1] his master had well noted
his absence, he had[2] returned with a little sponge and a
95 basin and had begun sopping up the waters of the Jordan
as though they had been a common slop.

"I'll filter it, Sir,"[3] said Gelstrap meekly. "It'll come
quite clean."[4]

Mr Pontifex saw hope in this suggestion, which was
100 shortly carried out under his own eyes by the help of a
piece of blotting paper and a funnel. Eventually it was
found that half a pint was saved, and this was held to be
sufficient.

VI

In this passage (from Chapter 18, Collins New Classics p. 92),
Butler introduces the adult Alethea Pontifex, the character
based on his friend, Miss Savage. Because of its hesitancy it
makes another good piece on which to practise one's skill at
reconstruction.

None of the Pontifexes were[5] deficient in good looks;
they were a well grown shapely family enough, but
Alethea was ~~the~~ ~~only~~ ~~one~~ ~~who~~ ~~far~~ the flower of the flock
even as regards good looks, while in respect of all other

[1] I.e., semi-colon was made into full stop and 'b' into 'B'.

[2] 'had' deleted in published text.

[3, 4] These two speeches were deleted and then reinstated—as if Butler
had thought of using some other remarks and then changed his mind.

[5] One of the occasional cases where both author and editors have
overlooked necessary alterations.

5   qualities that make a woman lovable, it seemed as though
the stock that had been intended for the three daughters,
and would have been about sufficient for them had all been
allotted to herself, her sisters getting none and she all.[1]

    It is impossible for me to explain how it was that she

10   and I never married. ~~She and I both~~ We two knew exceed-
ingly well, and that must suffice for the reader. There was
the most perfect sympathy and understanding between
us; ~~it was perfectly~~ we knew ~~very well~~ that neither of us
would marry any one else. ~~and she knew that~~ I ~~was~~

15   had asked her to marry me a dozen times over; ~~and~~
having said this much I ~~must leave this matter the~~ will
say no more, ~~for any explanation of which would have to
be very long to be intelligible would have to be long if
it were to be made intelligible, and~~ upon a point which is

20   in no way necessary for the development of my ~~present~~
story.

VII

From Chapter 34 (Collins New Classics p. 154), this passage
describes Aunt Alethea's concern for Ernest when he first went
to his public school.

    Miss Pontifex soon found out that Ernest did not like
games—but she saw also that he could hardly be expected
to like them. He was perfectly well shaped but unusually
devoid of physical muscular strength.[2] He got a fair share

5   of this in after life, but it came much later with him than
with other boys and at the time ~~I write of~~ of which I am
writing he was a mere little skeleton. He wanted something to develop his arms and chest without knocking
him about as much as the school games did. To supply this

---

[1] See note 5, p. 105.
[2] 'muscular' deleted in published text.

10 want ~~was Alethea's first anxiety~~. by some means which
should add also to his pleasures[1] was Alethea's first
anxiety. ~~It seemed to her that carpentry would be about~~
~~the sort of thing that would do for him, but she did not~~
~~like to propose it for fear of making him think that she~~
15 ~~too was like every one else anxious to make him do things~~
~~for his good which he disliked doing~~.[2] Rowing would have
answered every purpose, but unfortunately there was no
river at Roughborough.
     Whatever it was to be it must be something which he
20 should[3] ~~take a fancy to and~~ like as much as other boys liked
cricket or football, and ~~it must appear to him as though~~
he must think the wish for it ~~had~~ to have come originally
from himself; ~~and this was not so easy to hit upon~~ it was
not very easy to find anything that would do, but ere long
25 it occurred to her that she might enlist ~~Ernest's~~ his love of
music on her side, and asked him one ~~night~~ day when he
was spending a half holiday at her house whether he
would like ~~to have~~ her to buy an organ ~~of his own~~ for him
to play on. Of course the boy said yes; ~~and~~ then she told
30 him about her grandfather and the ~~organs~~[4] organs ~~which~~
he had built ~~for himself; and so fired his imagination~~ . It
had never entered into his head that he could make one,
but when he gathered ~~that thi~~ from what his aunt had said
that this was not out of the question, he rose as eagerly to
35 the bait as ~~his aunt~~ she could have desired and wanted to
begin learning to saw and plane so that he might make
the wooden pipes at once.
     Miss Pontifex ~~was much pleased, she~~ did not see how

---

[1] 'pleasure' in published text.

[2] 'doing' crossed out before the rest.

[3] 'would' in published text.

[4] First 'organs', then the deletion of 's', then the full deletion and the
substitution of 'organs'.

she could well have hit upon anything more suitable.
40 ~~Rowing would have done but there was no river at Roughborough~~ ,[1] and she liked also[2] the idea that he would incidentally get a knowledge of carpentering, for she was impressed, perhaps foolishly, with the wisdom of the German custom which gives every boy a handicraft of
45 some sort; ~~but she kept this source of pleasure carefully to herself, for she was above all things anxious to avoid his thinking that she wanted him to do things that would be of use to him. Her main idea was to amuse and interest him and help him to a little more muscular development.~~

[1] Comma formed from previous full-stop.
[2] 'also' deleted in published text.

Thomas Hardy

THE extracts in this section are taken from the manuscript of *Tess of the D'Urbervilles*, which is in the British Museum (Add. MS. 38,182), usually on exhibition.

Perhaps of all the novelists represented here Hardy poses the greatest problems, with his tremendous tumbles from the sublime to the ridiculous, or, to be more exact—for these weren't always entirely accidental—his switches from great poetry to the heaviest, most contrived melodrama, sometimes within a single page. It may be useful, therefore, to remember two facts when considering his alterations: that he did not at first take his novel-writing very seriously, and that he had certain highly idiosyncratic views about style.

Many of his novels were conceived and written originally as popular magazine serials, and with the earlier ones there is ample evidence to suggest that it wasn't until he had completed them in this form, having made the customary concessions to what various editors considered to be popular taste, that he saw their possibilities and tried to do justice to them as works of art. Writing of Hardy's changes in and to the serial version of *The Return of the Native*, John Paterson has given a clear summary of this process: 'The first edition represents, then, an important milestone in the history of *The Return of the Native*. For, if it failed to incorporate new levels of feeling and insight, if it failed to elaborate on and enrichen the substance of the novel, it sought to accomplish what was even more necessary at this point to its survival as a work of art: it sought to counteract the damaging influences of haste, pressure and censorship which had conspired, in the moment of the creative act itself, to undo it. The original damage was of course too fundamental to be easily repaired. However, whatever could be done at this late date to do justice to the novel, Hardy was very evidently concerned to do. Some seventeen years later, in fact, when he reëxamined the text for its publication as the sixth volume of the Uniform Edition, he could still strive to bring *The Return of the Native* closer to that "ideal" novel whose achievement the crippling restrictions of magazine publication had prevented.'[1]

The Return of the Native was first published as a book in 1878, *Tess of the D'Urbervilles* in 1891, and during the intervening years Hardy developed a technique of compromise with which he hoped to minimize the damage at the very outset—even to the extent of writing into his manuscripts at various crucial points the necessary magazine/volume alternatives. Whether this was satisfactory or not only a reading of the novels themselves can enable one to decide, but a study of the following extracts will certainly give some idea of the violent nature of the contortions that such a compromise often called for.

As for Hardy's views on style, let him speak for himself: 'The whole secret of a living style and the difference between it and a dead style, lies in not having too much style—being in fact, a little careless, or rather seeming to be, here and there. It brings wonderful life into the writing . . . Otherwise your style is like worn half-pence—all the fresh images rounded off by rubbing, and no crispness or movement at all. It is, of course, simply a carrying into prose the knowledge I have acquired in poetry—that inexact rhymes and rhythms now and then are

---

[1] *The Making of* The Return of the Native. John Paterson. University of California Press.

far more pleasing than correct ones.' And: 'So, then, if Nature's defects must be looked in the face and transcribed, whence arises the *art* in poetry and novel-writing? which must certainly show art, or it becomes merely mechanical reporting. I think the art lies in making these defects the basis of a hitherto unperceived beauty, by irradiating them with "the light that never was" on their surface, but is seen to be latent in them by the spiritual eye.'[1]

The draft was written in ink on one side only of large unlined sheets of paper. The handwriting is very clear, neat and firm. The margins are wide and, although unruled, remarkably straight. In places there is evidence of pencilled alterations—sometimes erased, sometimes inked over—but most of the numerous changes were made directly in ink. Any large insertion was usually written out on the back of the preceding page. As will have been gathered already, further changes were often made at stages between the manuscript and the final volume edition. Where these are trivial (e.g., concerning minor details of punctuation) I have stuck to the manuscript version without comment. Otherwise I have drawn attention to them, usually in footnotes.

I

Not all Hardy's manuscript changes were concerned with the serial/volume difficulties and stylistic theories, of course. Many of them were simply the outcome of the novelist's basic preoccupations with such things as timing, point of view and the presentation of character. This first passage, from Chapter 6 (Collins Classics pp. 67–69), contains some interesting alterations of this kind. It describes Tess's return from her visit to her 'kinswoman', Mrs d'Urberville. Her mother is full of

[1] Quoted from various sources by Morton Dauwen Zabel in *Craft and Character in Modern Fiction*. Gollancz.

romantically optimistic notions about the outcome, but Tess
herself is still rather perturbed by Alec d'Urberville's over-
familiar manner.

This is a complete scene (it is immediately followed by the
words 'A week afterwards'), and particular attention should be
paid to the difference Hardy's changes make to the way it ends.

> When she entered the house she perceived in a moment
> from her mother's triumphant manner that something
> had occurred in the interim.
>
> "Oh yes—I know all about it. I told you[1] it would be all
> 5   right, and now 'tis proved!"
>
> "Since I've been away? What has?" said Tess rather
> wearily.
>
> Her mother surveyed the girl up and down with arch
> approval, and went on banteringly, "So You've brought
> 10 'em round!"
>
> "How d'you know, mother?"
>
> "I've had a letter."
>
> Tess then remembered that there would have been
> just[2] time for this.
>
> 15   "They say—Mrs D'urberville[3] says—that she wants
> you to look after a little poultry-farm[4] which is her hobby.
> But this is only her artful way of getting you[5] there with-
> out raising your hopes. She's going to acknowledge[6]
> 'ee as kin—that's the meaning o't."
>
> 20   "But I didn't see her."

---

[1] "ee' in published text. (By 'published text' here and elsewhere in the notes, I mean that of the final volume edition.)

[2] 'just' deleted in published text.

[3] 'D'' superimposed on 'T'. In the early chapters of the MS. Hardy showed great indecision about the name. I shall now show only the final form throughout.

[4] 'fowl-farm' in published text.

[5] "ee' in published text.

[6] 'own' in published text.

"You ~~saw~~ zid somebody I suppose?"

"I saw her son."

"And did he acknowledge[1] 'ee?"

"Well—he called me Coz."

25   "Ah—[2] I knew it! . . . Jacky—he called her Coz!" cried Joan to her husband. "Well, he spoke to his mother, of course, and she da[3] wants ~~y~~ 'ee there."

    "But ~~I didn' see her.~~ ~~And~~ I don't know that I am apt at managing[4] fowls," said the ~~surprized~~ dubious Tess.

30   "Then I don't know who is apt. You've ~~been~~ ben born in the business, and brought up in it. Them that's[5] born in a business always know more about it than any ~~ap~~printice.[6] Besides, that's only just a show of something for you to do, that you ~~may~~midn't feel dependent."

35   "I don't altogether think I ought to go," said Tess thoughtfully. "Who wrote the letter? Will you let me look at it?"

    "Mrs d'Urberville wrote it. Here it is."

    The letter was in the third person, and briefly informed
40 Mrs ~~Trouble~~Durbeyfield[7] that her daughter's services would be useful to that lady in the management of her poultry-farm, ~~and~~ that ~~a~~ a comfortable room~~s~~ would be provided for her if she could come, and that the emolument[8] would be on a liberal scale if they liked her.

45   "O—that's all," said Tess.

---

[1] 'own' in published text.

[2] 'Ah—' changed to 'An'' in published text.

[3] 'do' in published text.

[4] 'tending' in published text.

[5] 'They that be' in published text.

[6] ''printice' in published text.

[7] 'Durbey' superimposed on 'Trouble'. 'Troublefield' was obviously the name Hardy thought of using to correspond with the original 'Turberville'. Again I shall show only the final form in future.

[8] 'wages' in published text.

"You couldn't expect her to throw her arms round ~~you~~ 'ee, an' to kiss and to coll 'ee all at once."

Tess looked out of the window.

"I would rather stay here with father and you," ~~said~~ 50 ~~Tess~~ she said nervously reflecting.[1]

"But why?"

"I'd rather not tell you why, mother—indeed I don't quite know why."

II

From Chapter 8 (Collins Classics p. 78). The occasion is that of Tess's being met by Alec on her way to take up the appointment with his mother.

Here again Hardy is mainly concerned with one of the fundamentals of fiction-writing: in this case the problem of presenting vividly and accurately a rather complicated physical action. And again there is evidence of indecision about a name, 'Tess' having originally been 'Sue' and then 'Rose Mary'. 'Sue' presents difficulties of its own, as Hardy no doubt realized when writing in this passage 'The wind blew through Sue's white muslin to'—and, a few lines later, '"No, no!" said Sue. "Show more sense, do . . ."'

Down, down they ~~whizzed~~ sped, the wheels humming like a top, the dog-cart rocking right and left, ~~the and and advancing in~~ its axis acquiring[2] a slightly ~~diagonal~~ oblique ~~position bearing~~ set in relation to the line of pro-5 gress; the figure of the horse rising and falling in undulations before them.[3] Sometimes a wheel was off the

[1] 'nervously reflecting' deleted in published text.

[2] Thus Hardy, after striking out 'the' went on to write 'and acquiring . . .' etc. Then, at the end of the sentence—or later, during revision—after striking out the first 'and', he began to make an amendment beginning 'and advancing in', deleting it almost at once, even before he'd had time to cancel 'acquiring'. Finally he inserted 'its axis'.

[3] I.e., 'before them' was inserted first, then 'in undulations'.

ground, it seemed for many yards: sometimes a stone was sent spinning over the hedge, and flinty sparks from the horse's hoofs outshone the daylight. The fore-part[1]

10 of the straight road enlarged with their advance, ~~like an opening umbrella~~ a splitting stick, the two banks dividing like a splitting ~~abroad and like a~~ stick; and one ~~rush~~inged past at each shoulder.[2]

The wind blew through Tess's[3] white muslin to her very

15 skin, and her washed hair flew out behind. She was determined to show no open fear, but ~~skin, and she was so terrified that~~ she clutched d'Urberville's rein arm.

III

For many readers the book's creaking melodrama is redeemed by its poetry. This redemptive power works internally also, on the characters themselves. The following passage (the last paragraph of Chapter 10) is an example of this. The farm workers are returning tipsy from a village dance and there has been a brawl, from which Tess has been rescued by the passing Alec d'Urberville, who gives her a lift. "Out of the frying-pan into the fire!" reflects one of the brawlers.

And then[4] these children of the open air, whom even alcohol[5] could scarce injure permanently, betook themselves to the field-path; and as they went there moved

---

[1] 'aspect' in published text.

[2] Probable order: 1. 'like an opening umbrella, the two banks splitting abroad and rushing past at each shoulder.' 2. 'like a splitting stick, the two banks'—after which Hardy must have checked and gone on to 3. '... advance, the two banks splitting like a stick; and one rushed past at each shoulder.' 4. 'the two banks dividing, like a splitting stick; and one ...' etc. Finally, in the published text, the last clause becomes '; one rushing past at each shoulder.'

[3] Originally 'Sue's', then 'Rose Mary's' before final version. Another recurring series which I shall generally ignore.

[4] 'Then' in published text.

[5] 'even excess of alcohol' in published text.

onward with them, around the shadow of each one's head,
5   an opalized circle or glory,[1] formed by the moon's rays
upon the glistening sheet of dew. Each ~~traveller~~ pedestrian
could see no halo but his or her own, which never deserted
~~the his shade~~ the head-shadow whatever its vulgar
unsteadiness might be; but adhered to it, and persistently
10   beautified it; till the erratic motion[2] ~~seemed appeared to
be~~ seemed an inherent part of the ~~scene, and of Nature,
and of the time~~. irradiation[3] and the fumes of their breathing a component of the night-mist:[4] and the spirit of the
scene, and of the moonlight, and of Nature, seemed
15   harmoniously to mingle with the spirit of wine.

IV

We come now to one of the book's most crucial passages: the
seduction scene in Chapter 11. Here the great popular-serial/
novel conflict is very much in evidence—and not only in the
manuscript, for many readers of the book must have found this
incident critically disturbing to their 'willing suspension of dis-
belief' because of the inconsistencies created by that conflict.
Given Alec d'Urberville as the rather ludicrously obnoxious
upstart that Hardy makes of him most of the time, it is almost
impossible to imagine even a very tired Tess succumbing to
him, for Alec is never accused of having employed violence. Of
course, there could have been other artificial aids . . . a drug,
perhaps . . . or drink . . . As this passage shows, Hardy certainly
hadn't overlooked such a possibility. Nor had he overlooked
what is probably the only really artistically and psychologically
valid alternative: making Alec less of a cardboard villain and

---

[1] In published text, 'an opalized . . . glory' becomes 'a circle of opalized light'.

[2] 'motions' in published text.

[3] Punctuation point after 'irradiation' obliterated by insertion mark. Published text gives a comma.

[4] 'night's mist' in published text.

more of a human being, not unattractive and not entirely selfish. Here and there, through the alterations, glimpses of a more sympathetic attitude towards this character can be caught.

Most of the published variations are so important that I have integrated them with the manuscript text between square brackets, instead of showing them in footnotes. As usual, minor punctuation changes and alterations of names are not shown.

He turned the horse's head into the ~~ditch~~ bushes, hitched ~~the~~ bridle ~~reins round~~ him on to a ~~stake~~ bough, and hauling down the ~~apron of~~ rug from the vehicle spread it upon the thick leaves. [*Printed text after* 'bough' *reads*:
5 'and made a sort of couch or nest for her in the deep mass of dead leaves.']¹ "Now you sit there," he said. "That will keep away the damp. ["The leaves have not got damp as yet.] Just ~~have~~ give an eye to the horse—it will be quite sufficient."
10 He took a few steps away from her, but returning said, "By the bye, Tess; your father has a new ~~cart~~ horse [cob] today. Somebody gave it to him."

"Somebody? You!"

D'Urberville nodded.
15 "O how very good of you that is!" she exclaimed with a painful sense of the awkwardness of having to thank him just then.

"And the children have some toys."

"I didn't know—you ever sent them anything!" she
20 murmured, much moved. "I almost wish you had not—yes, I almost wish it!"

"Why, dear?"

"It—hampers me so."

¹ Hardy had already discarded the vehicle in the previous chapter, having Alec ride up to the brawlers on horseback—though this was probably done retrospectively.

"Tess [Tessy]—don't you love me ever so little now?"

25   "I am grateful," she reluctantly admitted. "But I fear I do not—" The sudden vision of his passion for herself as a factor in this result so distressed her that, beginning with one slow tear, and then following with another, she wept outright.

30   "Don't cry, dear, dear Tess [one]! Now sit down here, and wait till I come." She passively sat down on the red rug that he had spread, ['amid the leaves he had heaped' *for* 'on the . . . spread'] and shivered slightly. "Are you cold?" he asked.

35   "Not very—a little."

He touched her with his fingers, which sank into her as into ~~a billow froth~~ a billow.[1] ['down' *for* 'a billow'] "You have only that puffy muslin dress on—how's that?"

"It is my best summer one. 'Twas very warm when I
40 started, and I didn't know I was going to ride,[2] and that it would be night."

"Nights are [grow] chilly in September. Let me see." He went to the gig, took a ~~bottle~~ a large wicker-cased jar from under the seat, and after some trouble in ~~uncorking~~
45 ~~it~~ opening it with a pocket corkscrew held it to her mouth unawares. Tess sputtered and coughed and ~~gasping~~ "It will go on my pretty frock!" swallowed as he poured, to prevent the catastrophe she feared. "That's it— now you'll feel warmer," said d'Urberville, with much
50 satisfaction, as he restored the ~~bottle~~ jar to its place. "It is ~~my mother's household spirit jar, but she won't know~~ a two-gallon jar of spirits that my mother ordered me to bring for household purposes, and she won't mind my

---

[1] Actually 'a billow' was crossed out and 'froth' inserted in pencil, this being rubbed out later.

[2] Originally intended to be end of speech, 'and' being superimposed on final stop and end quotation marks.

using some of it medicinally. [*Published text from* "'Let
55 me see.'" *reads*: 'He pulled off a light overcoat that he had
worn, and put it round her tenderly. "That's it—now
you'll feel warmer," he continued.'] Now my pretty, rest
there; I shall soon be back again."

He [Having buttoned the overcoat round her shoulders
60 he] plunged ~~amid~~ into the webs of vapour which [by this
time] ~~hung about~~ ~~spread~~ formed veils between the trees,
and she could hear the rustling of the branches as he
ascended the adjoining slope, till his movements were no
louder than the hopping of a bird, and finally died away.
65 With the setting of the moon the pale light lessened, and
Tess became invisible as she fell into reverie upon the
~~crimson~~ red[1] rug ['leaves' *for* 'red rug'] where he had left
her.

In the meantime d'Urberville [Alec] had pushed on up
70 the slope to clear up his [genuine] doubt as to the locality
['quarter of the Chase' *for* 'locality'] they were in. He
had, in fact, driven [ridden] quite at random for two
hours, [over an hour,] taking any turning that came to
hand in order to prolong the drive ['companionship' *for*
75 'the drive'] with her, and giving far more attention to
Tess's ~~face~~ ~~beauty~~ person [moonlit person] than to any
wayside object. A little rest for the jaded animal being
desirable he did not hasten his search for ~~information~~
landmarks. ~~The~~ ~~summit~~ ~~of~~ A clamber over the hill into
80 the adjoining vale brought him to the fence of a highway
whose aspect [contours] he recognised, which settled the
question of their whereabouts. D'Urberville thereupon
turned back; but by this time the moon had quite gone
down, and, ~~owing to~~ partly on account of the fog, ~~the~~
85 ~~wood~~ ~~Chase~~ ~~was a a~~ the Chase was ~~now~~ wrapped in thick

---

[1] 'crimson' first inserted in pencil, then erased and replaced in ink by
'red'.

~~darkness had descended upon the Chase~~ darkness, although morning was not far off. He was obliged to
advance with outstretched hands, to avoid contact
with the boughs, and discovered that to hit the exact
90 spot from which he had started was at first entirely
beyond him. Roaming up and down, round and round, he
at length heard a slight movement of the horse close at
hand; and the rug [sleeve of his overcoat] unexpectedly
caught his foot.

95   "Tess!" said d'Urberville.

There was no answer, ~~and the~~ . The ~~blackness~~ obscurity
was now so intense that he could see absolutely nothing.
The red rug, and the white muslin figure he had left upon it
were now all blackness alike. ~~He Hawnferne[1]~~ He stooped,
100 and heard a gentle regular breathing. She was sleeping
soundly. He knelt and bent lower, and her breath
~~touched~~ warmed his face, and in a moment his cheek was
in contact with hers and with her hair, and her eyes.
~~She[2] was sleeping soundly; and there was damp about her~~
105 A ~~damp~~ wetness accompanied the touch ——[3] of her eye
lashes upon his face as if she had wept.

~~There was nothing but silence around.~~

Darkness and silence ruled everywhere around.

[In the published text, from 'no answer' *to* 'Darkness . . .',
110 *the passage reads*: 'The obscurity was now so great that he
could see absolutely nothing but a pale nebulousness at
his feet, which represented the white muslin figure he had
left upon the dead leaves. Everything else was blackness
alike. D'Urberville stooped; and heard a gentle regular
115 breathing. He knelt and bent lower, till her breath warmed
his face, and in a moment his cheek was in contact with

[1] Another of the pre-d'Urberville surnames.
[2] Could have been 'Sue'.
[3] Indistinguishable word deleted.

hers. She was sleeping soundly, and upon her eyelashes there lingered tears.']

V

Finally, from the beginning of Chapter 14, comes one of those long descriptions of farm work that do much to make the book so memorable. Here we see the poetry being drawn from rather than cast over or injected into an agricultural process—partly deliberately, with the help of the sun, but mainly perhaps as a result of the author's chief concern (shown in the multiplicity of his adjustments and readjustments) simply to give a perfectly clear picture of what is happening.

It was a hazy sunrise in August. The nocturnal vapours,[1] attacked by the warm beams, divided and shrank themselves ~~away to detached~~ apart into isolated fleeces ~~or~~ and layers of white in hollows and coverts,[2]
5 where they ~~wasted into nothing~~ waited till they should be dried ~~into~~ away to nothing.[3]

The sun, on account of the mist, had a curious, sentient, personal look, demanding the masculine pronoun for its adequate expression. His present aspect, coupled with
10 the absence[4] of all human forms from[5] the scene, explained the ~~old-time~~ primitive[6] heliolatries in one[7] moment. The

[1] 'denser nocturnal vapours' in published text.

[2] In published text, 'divided and . . . coverts' clause reads: 'were dividing and shrinking into isolated fleeces within hollows and coverts.'

[3] Change made thus: 'into nothing', original end of sentence, deleted; 'wasted' altered to 'waited' by making 's' an 'i'; and 'till . . . nothing' added.

[4] 'lack' in p.t.

[5] 'in' in p.t.

[6] 'old-time' in p.t.

[7] 'a' in p.t.

observer[1] could feel that a saner religion had never pre-
vailed under the sky. The luminary was ~~the head of~~ a
golden-haired, ~~beaming-faced~~, ~~mild~~ardent-eyed, godlike
15 creature,[2] gazing down in the vigour and intentness of
youth upon an earth that ~~was not without~~ <u>was brimming
with interest</u> for him.

His light <u>a little later</u> broke through chinks and joints[3]
of cottage shutters, throwing stripes like red-hot pokers
20 upon cupboards, chests of drawers, and other furniture
within; and awakening harvesters who were not already
astir. They feared that ——[4] <u>fruity</u> colour might mean
an uncertain day.[5]

But of all red[6] things that morning the reddest[7] were
25 two broad flat[8] arms of <u>painted</u> wood which rose from
the margin of a yellow cornfield hard by Marlott village.
They ~~were the blades of~~ with two others hidden by the
corn, formed the large[9] revolving <u>Maltese</u> cross of the
reaping-machine, which had been <u>brought</u> to the field on
30 the previous evening, to be ready for operations early[10]
this day. The crimson[11] paint with which they were
coloured,[12] intensified in hue by the toned[13] sunlight, ~~gave~~

---

[1] 'One' for 'The observer' in p.t.

[2] 'golden-haired, beaming, mild-eyed, God-like creature' in p.t. In
MS., 'being' tentatively inserted above 'creature' in pencil, then erased.

[3] 'and joints' deleted in p.t.

[4] Deleted word or part of word indistinguishable. Might have been
'col'.

[5] 'They feared . . . day.' deleted in p.t.

[6] 'ruddy' in p.t.

[7] 'brightest' in p.t.

[8] 'flat' deleted in p.t.

[9] Alteration made thus: 'the blades of' deleted, 'with' superimposed
on 'were' and 'two others . . . large' inserted. In the p.t. this became
'They, with two others below, formed the revolving . . .' with 'large'
deleted.

[10] 'early' deleted in p.t.   [11] 'crimson' deleted in p.t.

[12] 'smeared' for 'coloured' in p.t.   [13] 'toned' deleted in p.t.

imparted to them ~~the~~ an appearance[1] of having been dipped in gore.[2]

35 The field had already been "opened"; that is to say, a lane a few feet wide had been hand-cut through the wheat along the whole circumference of the field, for the first passage of the horses and machine.

~~At six o' clock~~ tTwo groups, one of men and lads, the
40 other of women, ~~came~~ had come down the lane just at the hour when the shadows of the ~~east~~ eastern hedge-top struck the ~~other~~ west hedge midway, ~~and~~ ~~prevented~~ veiling the interior of the lane as yet;[3] so that the heads of the groups were ~~in~~ ~~sunlight~~ ~~and~~ enjoying sunrise while
45 their ~~bodies~~ feet were still in the dawn. They disappeared from the lane between the two stone posts which flanked the nearest field-gate.

Presently there arose from within a ticking like the love-~~making~~ call[4] of the grasshopper, which told that the
50 machine had begun,[5] and a moving ~~procession~~ concatenation[6] was visible over the gate, ~~the~~ a driver sitting upon one of the hauling horses, and ~~the~~ an attendant on the seat of the implement. ~~Round and round~~ ~~Down~~ Along one side of the field ~~they~~ the whole wain went, the
55 ~~red~~[7] arms of the mechanical reaper revolving slowly, ~~now~~ ~~passing~~ till it passed down the hill quite out of sight, ~~then~~ ~~coming~~ . In a minute it ~~came~~ was heard coming[8] up on the other ~~hand~~ side of the field at the same equable

[1] 'a look' for 'an appearance' in p.t.

[2] 'liquid fire' for 'gore' in p.t.

[3] 'veiling . . . as yet;' deleted in p.t.

[4] Alteration made in pencil; p.t. reverts to 'love-making'.

[5] 'which told that' deleted in p.t. and new sentence begun with 'The machine . . .'.

[6] Followed in p.t. by 'of three horses and the aforesaid long rickety machine'.

[7] 'red' deleted in p.t.

[8] 'In a minute it came' in p.t.

pace; ~~the and a~~ the glistening brass star in the forehead
60 of the fore-horse ~~first catching~~ <u>suddenly caught</u>[1] the eye
as it rose into view over the stubble, then the red arms
popped up, and then the whole machine.[2]

The originally[3] narrow lane of stubble encircling[4] the
field grew wider with each circuit, and the standing corn
65 was reduced to smaller and smaller[5] area as the morning
wore on. Rabbits, hares, snakes, rats, mice, all[6] retreated
inwards as into a fastness, unaware of the ephemeral
nature of that[7] refuge, and of the doom that awaited
them later in the day when, their covert shrinking to a
70 more and more horrible narrowness, ~~and~~ they were all[8]
huddled together friends and foes, <u>till</u> the last few yards
of upright wheat ~~became ener~~ fell <u>also</u> under the teeth of
the ~~unerring~~ machine,[9] and they were ~~all~~ <u>every one</u> put to
a fearful[10] death by the sticks and stones of the harvesters.
75 The reaping-machine left the fallen corn behind it in
little heaps, each heap being of the quantity for a sheaf;
and upon these the <u>active</u> binders <u>in the rear</u> laid their
hands—<u>mainly women, but</u> some of them men in print
shirts and corduroy[11] trousers supported ~~by leather straps~~
80 round their waists <u>by leather straps</u>[12] ~~which, rendering~~

[1] P.t. reverts to 'first catching'.
[2] In p.t. after 'stubble,': 'then the bright arms, and then the whole machine.'.
[3] 'originally' deleted in p.t.
[4] 'encompassing' in p.t.
[5] 'and smaller' deleted in p.t.
[6] 'all' deleted in p.t.
[7] 'their' in p.t.
[8] 'all' deleted in p.t.
[9] 'unerring' crossed out in pencil but retained in p.t., where 'reaper' is substituted for 'machine'.
[10] 'a fearful' deleted in p.t.
[11] 'corduroy' deleted in p.t.
[12] Alteration made by usual transposition mark.

~~which rendered~~ <u>rendering</u>[1] useless the two <u>brace-buttons[2]</u> behind; ~~so that~~ ~~they sh~~ ~~twinkled~~ ~~and~~ ~~glared~~ ~~at~~ ~~every~~ ~~their~~ ~~only~~ ~~seeming~~ ~~purpose~~ ~~was~~ ~~being~~ ~~to~~ <u>which</u> twinkled and ~~glare~~ <u>bristled with sunbeams</u> at every <u>movement o̅f the</u>[3]

85   wearer, as if they were a pair of eyes in the small of his back.[4]

[1] Alteration made by first crossing out comma and superimposing 'ed' on 'ing', then crossing out resulting 'which rendered' and inserting 'rendering'.

[2] 'brace-' deleted in p.t.

[3] 'each' in p.t.

[4] The evident order of alteration here was: 1. 'sh'—probably the beginning of 'shone'—deleted; 2. 'they twinkled and glared at every' deleted; 3. the construction 'so that their only seeming purpose was to twinkle and glare' begun; 4. 'so that' deleted and 'being' substituted for 'was'; 5. then as above.

Henry James

The Portrait of a Lady, which was first published in 1881, was
revised by the author some twenty-five years later when pre-
paring his novels and stories for the definitive New York edition.
The changes were not sweeping. There were no great shifts of
attitude reflected in them. They were indeed chiefly stylistic.
But their total effect was one of greater penetration. They
tended cumulatively (for physically they were mainly small readjustments) to give greater insight into the personalities and
motives of the principal characters, and by doing so they gave
the book a keener moral bite.

They did none of this directly, however. They were never in
the form of snippets of extra information. What James did was
—principally—to enrich the imagery, sometimes by introducing fresh, vividly revealing figures, sometimes by sharpening
and rearranging those already there, sometimes by introducing
a thread of imagery that was to run through the book and
become a sort of string from which he could pluck a certain
key-note.

Through the imagery, too—and by certain other kinds of
small readjustments—James very subtly heightened the drama
in many places, no doubt drawing on his experience, artistically
and financially disastrous but technically valuable, of writing
for the stage in the years between the novel's first publication

and its revision. Some of the images introduced are in fact directly drawn from the theatre, just as many others reflect James's equally great, though non-participating love of painting, as F. O. Matthiessen points out, in the chapter on *The Portrait of a Lady* and its alterations, in *Henry James: The Major Phase*.

James has been criticized for the triviality of many of the changes he made, for what some have considered to be mere stylistic tinkering and wordy over-elaboration. Here and there the charge is justified, but I feel that on the whole the changes vastly improved the book. Again, there are some who tend to speak of the novels of James's middle period (of which this is one) as being far superior to what they consider to be the too ornate, too elaborately synthetic nature of the products of his late period; and I cannot help wondering if these critics appreciate how much the earlier novels gained as a result of the changes made by the 'later' James.

However, these are only my opinions. Before considering the following specimens the reader would do well to consult Matthiessen's book and of course read or re-read the novel itself. And for further study—of a most fascinating and fruitful kind— I would strongly recommend a reading of all the earlier editions of the novels and stories in the light of their revision.

I

This passage, describing the heroine's first suitor, Caspar Goodwood, comes from Chapter 13. The changes should be considered in relation to Goodwood's somewhat emblematic function in the book and the contrast his character forms with that of Gilbert Osmond, whom the girl eventually marries.

Henry James

He was the son of a proprietor of certain well-known cotton-mills in Massachusetts—a gentleman who had accumulated a considerable fortune in the exercise of this industry. Caspar now managed the establishment, with a
5 judgement and a brilliancy which, in spite of keen competition and languid years, had kept its prosperity from dwindling. He had received the better part of his education at Harvard University, where, however, he had gained more renown as a gymnast and an oarsman than as a
10 votary of culture. Later, he had become reconciled to culture, and though he was still fond of sport, he was capable of showing an excellent understanding of other matters. He had a remarkable aptitude for mechanics, and had invented an improvement in the cotton-spinning
15 process, which was now largely used and was known by his name. You might have seen his name in the papers in connection with this fruitful contrivance; assurance of which he had given to Isabel by showing her in the columns of the New York *Interviewer* an exhaustive
20 article on the Goodwood patent—an article not prepared by Miss Stackpole, friendly as she had proved herself to his more sentimental interests. He had a great talent for business, for administration, and for making people execute his purpose and carry out his views—for managing
25 men, as the phrase was; and to give its complete value to this faculty, he had an insatiable, an almost fierce, ambition. It always struck people who knew him that he might do greater things than carry on a cotton-factory; there was nothing cottony about Caspar Goodwood, and
30 his friends took for granted that he would not always content himself with that. He had once said to Isabel that, if the United States were only not such a confoundedly

The Portrait of a Lady

He was the son of a proprietor of well-known cotton-
mills in Massachusetts—a gentleman who had accumulated a considerable fortune in the exercise of this industry.
Caspar at present managed the works, and with a judge-
5 ment and a temper which, in spite of keen competition
and languid years, had kept their prosperity from
dwindling. He had received the better part of his education at Harvard College, where, however, he had gained
renown rather as a gymnast and an oarsman than as a
10 gleaner of more dispersed knowledge. Later on he had
learned that the finer intelligence too could vault and pull
and strain—might even, breaking the record, treat itself
to rare exploits. He had thus discovered in himself a
sharp eye for the mystery of mechanics, and had in-
15 vented an improvement in the cotton-spinning process
which was now largely used and was known by his name.
You might have seen it in the newspapers in connexion
with this fruitful contrivance; assurance of which he had
given to Isabel by showing her in the columns of the New
20 York *Interviewer* an exhaustive article on the Goodwood
patent—an article not prepared by Miss Stackpole,
friendly as she had proved herself to his more sentimental
interests. There were intricate, bristling things he rejoiced
in; he liked to organize, to contend, to administer; he
25 could make people work his will, believe in him, march
before him and justify him. This was the art, as they said,
of managing men—which rested, in him, further, on a
bold though brooding ambition. It struck those who
knew him well that he might do greater things than carry
30 on a cotton factory; there was nothing cottony about
Caspar Goodwood, and his friends took for granted that he
would somehow and somewhere write himself in bigger

peaceful nation, he would find his proper place in the
army. He keenly regretted that the Civil War should have
35 terminated just as he had grown old enough to wear
shoulder-straps, and was sure that if something of the
same kind would only occur again, he would make a
display of striking military talent. It pleased Isabel to
believe that he had the qualities of a famous captain, and
40 she answered that, if it would help him on, she shouldn't
object to a war—a speech which ranked among the three
or four most encouraging ones he had elicited from her,
and of which the value was not diminished by her subsequent regret at having said anything so heartless, inas-
45 much as she never communicated this regret to him. She
liked at any rate this idea of his being potentially a
commander of men—liked it much better than some
other points in his character and appearance. She cared
nothing about his cotton-mill, and the Goodwood patent
50 left her imagination absolutely cold. She wished him
not an inch less a man than he was; but she sometimes
thought he would be rather nicer if he looked, for instance,
a little differently. His jaw was too square and grim,
and his figure too straight and stiff; these things sug-
55 gested a want of easy adaptability to some of the occasions
of life. Then she regarded with disfavour a habit he had of
dressing always in the same manner; it was not apparently
that he wore the same clothes continually, for, on the
contrary, his garments had a way of looking rather too
60 new. But they all seemed to be made of the same piece;
the pattern, the cut, was in every case identical. She had
reminded herself more than once that this was a frivolous
objection to a man of Mr Goodwood's importance; and
then she had amended the rebuke by saying that it would
65 be a frivolous objection if she were in love with him.
She was not in love with him, and therefore she might

letters. But it was as if something large and confused, something dark and ugly, would have to call upon him:
35 he was not after all in harmony with mere smug peace and greed and gain, an order of things of which the vital breath was ubiquitous advertisement. It pleased Isabel to believe that he might have ridden, on a plunging steed, the whirlwind of a great war—a war like the Civil strife
40 that had over-darkened her conscious childhood and his ripening youth.

She liked at any rate this idea of his being by character and in fact a mover of men—liked it much better than some other points in his nature and aspect. She cared
45 nothing for his cotton mill—the Goodwood patent left her imagination absolutely cold. She wished him no ounce less of his manhood, but she sometimes thought he would be rather nicer if he looked, for instance, a little differently. His jaw was too square and set and his figure
50 too straight and stiff: these things suggested a want of easy consonance with the deeper rhythms of life. Then she viewed with reserve a habit he had of dressing always in the same manner; it was not apparently that he wore the same clothes continually, for, on the contrary, his gar-
55 ments had a way of looking rather too new. But they all seemed of the same piece; the figure, the stuff, was so drearily usual. She had reminded herself more than once that this was a frivolous objection to a person of his importance; and then she had amended the rebuke by
60 saying that it would be a frivolous objection only if she were in love with him. She was not in love with him and therefore might criticize his small defects as well as his

criticise his small defects as well as his great ones—which
latter consisted in the collective reproach of his being too
serious, or, rather, not of his being too serious, for one
70 could never be that, but of his seeming so. He showed his
seriousness too simply, too artlessly; when one was alone
with him he talked too much about the same subject, and
when other people were present he talked too little about
anything. And yet he was the strongest man she had ever
75 known, and she believed that at bottom he was the clever-
est. It was very strange; she was far from understanding
the contradictions among her own impressions. Caspar
Goodwood had never corresponded to her idea of a delightful person, and she supposed that this was why he was
80 so unsatisfactory.

II

The following extracts, from Chapter 12, offer at least one
striking example of the sort of change usually objected to. But
they also, amongst other things, show how much deeper into
motives James's revisions penetrated.

Lord Warburton has just proposed marriage to Isabel and she
has promised to give an answer later.

1881 EDITION

He held out his hand, and she gave him hers a moment
—a moment long enough for him to bend his head and kiss
it. Then, shaking his hunting-whip with little quick
strokes, he walked rapidly away. He was evidently very
5 nervous.

Isabel herself was nervous, but she was not affected
as she would have imagined. What she felt was not a

great—which latter consisted in the collective reproach of
his being too serious, or, rather, not of his being so, since
65 one could never be, but certainly of his seeming so. He
showed his appetites and designs too simply and artlessly;
when one was alone with him he talked too much about
the same subject, and when other people were present
he talked too little about anything. And yet he was of
70 supremely strong, clean make—which was so much: she
saw the different fitted parts of him as she had seen, in
museums and portraits, the different fitted parts of
armoured warriors—in plates of steel handsomely inlaid
with gold. It was very strange: where, ever, was any
75 tangible link between her impression and her act?
Caspar Goodwood had never corresponded to her idea of
a delightful person, and she supposed that this was why
he left her so harshly critical.

REVISED TEXT (II)

He held out his hand, and she gave him hers a moment—
a moment long enough for him to bend his handsome bared
head and kiss it. Then, still agitating, in his mastered
emotion, his implement of the chase, he walked rapidly
5 away. He was evidently much upset.

Isabel herself was upset, but she had not been affected
as she would have imagined. What she felt was not a great

great responsibility, a great difficulty of choice; for it
appeared to her that there was no choice in the question.
10 She could not marry Lord Warburton; the idea failed to
correspond to any vision of happiness that she had
hitherto entertained, or was now capable of entertaining.
She must write this to him, she must convince him, and
this duty was comparatively simple. But what disturbed
15 her, in the sense that it struck her with wonderment, was
this very fact that it cost her so little to refuse a great
opportunity. With whatever qualifications one would,
Lord Warburton had offered her a great opportunity;
the situation might have discomforts, might contain
20 elements that would displease her, but she did her sex no
injustice in believing that nineteen women out of twenty
would accommodate themselves to it with extreme zeal.
Why then upon her also should it not impose itself?

III

From Chapter 23, in the account of Isabel's first meeting with
Osmond, we have several examples of the heightening of the
imagery, with dramatic and richly suggestive effect.

1881 EDITION

Gilbert Osmond came to see Madame Merle, who presented him to the young lady seated almost out of sight at
the other end of the room. Isabel, on this occasion, took
little share in the conversation; she scarcely even smiled
5 when the others turned to her appealingly; but sat there
as an impartial auditor of their brilliant discourse. Mrs
Touchett was not present, and these two had it their own

responsibility, a great difficulty of choice; it appeared
to her there had been no choice in the question. She
10   couldn't marry Lord Warburton; the idea failed to support
any enlightened prejudice in favour of the free explora-
tion of life that she had hitherto entertained or was now
capable of entertaining. She must write this to him, she
must convince him, and that duty was comparatively
15   simple. But what disturbed her, in the sense that it
struck her with wonderment, was this very fact that it
cost her so little to refuse a magnificent 'chance'. With
whatever qualifications one would, Lord Warburton had
offered her a great opportunity; the situation might have
20   discomforts, might contain oppressive, might contain
narrowing elements, might prove really but a stupifying
anodyne; but she did her sex no injustice in believing that
nineteen women out of twenty would have accommodated
themselves to it without a pang. Why then upon her also
25   should it not irresistibly impose itself?

REVISED TEXT (III)

Gilbert Osmond came to see Madame Merle, who presented him to the young lady lurking at the other side of
the room. Isabel took on this occasion little part in the
talk; she scarcely even smiled when the others turned to
5   her invitingly; she sat there as if she had been at the play
and had paid even a large sum for her place. Mrs Touchett
was not present, and these two had it, for the effect of

way. They talked extremely well; it struck Isabel almost
as a dramatic entertainment, rehearsed in advance.
10 Madame Merle referred everything to her, but the girl
answered nothing, though she knew that this attitude
would make Mr Osmond think she was one of those dull
people who bored him. It was the worse, too, that
Madame Merle would have told him she was almost as
15 much above the merely respectable average as he himself,
and that she was putting her friend dreadfully in the
wrong. But this was no matter, for once; even if more had
depended on it, Isabel could not have made an attempt
to shine. There was something in Mr Osmond that arrested
20 her and held her in suspense—made it seem more
important that she should get an impression of him than
that she should produce one herself. Besides, Isabel had
little skill in producing an impression which she knew to be
expected; nothing could be more charming, in general,
25 than to seem dazzling; but she had a perverse unwillingness to perform by arrangement. Mr Osmond, to do him
justice, had a well-bred air of expecting nothing; he was a
quiet gentleman, with a colourless manner, who said
elaborate things with a great deal of simplicity. Isabel,
30 however, privately perceived that if he did not expect, he
observed; she was very sure he was sensitive. His face, his
head were sensitive; he was not handsome, but he was
fine, as fine as one of the drawings in the long gallery
above the bridge, at the Uffizi. Mr Osmond was very
35 delicate; the tone of his voice alone would have proved it.
It was the visitor's delicacy that made her abstain from
interference. His talk was like the tinkling of glass, and if
she had put out her finger she might have changed the
pitch and spoiled the concert.

brilliancy, all their own way. They talked of the Florentine, the Roman, the cosmopolite world, and might
10 have been distinguished performers figuring for a charity. It all had the rich readiness that would have come from rehearsal. Madame Merle appealed to her as if she had been on the stage, but she could ignore any learnt cue without spoiling the scene; although of course she thus
15 put dreadfully in the wrong the friend who had told Mr Osmond she could be depended on. This was no matter for once; even if more had been involved she could have made no attempt to shine. There was something in the visitor that checked her and held her in suspense—made
20 it more important she should get an impression of him than that she should produce one herself. Besides, she had little skill in producing an impression which she knew to be expected: nothing could be happier, in general, than to seem dazzling, but she had a perverse unwillingness to
25 glitter by arrangement. Mr Osmond, to do him justice, had a well-bred air of expecting nothing, a quiet ease that covered everything, even the first show of his own wit. This was the more grateful as his face, his head, was sensitive; he was not handsome, but he was fine, as fine
30 as one of the drawings in the long gallery above the bridge of the Uffizi. And his very voice was fine—the more strangely that, with its clearness, it yet somehow wasn't sweet. This had had really to do with making her abstain from interference. His utterance was the vibration of
35 glass, and if she had put out her finger she might have changed the pitch and spoiled the concert.

IV

James was not solely concerned with imagery in his revisions, as will have been noticed in some of the foregoing examples. Where he felt it necessary he would tighten up the dialogue, making it more suggestive perhaps, or more natural, or more dramatic, or, through it, attempting to clarify an issue. What is the effect of the recasting in the following example, drawn from Chapter 27, where Osmond, Isabel, Lord Warburton and Isabel's cousin, Ralph Touchett, (who also is in love with her), meet in St Peter's?

1881 VERSION

"What's your opinion of St Peter's?" Mr Osmond asked of Isabel.

"It's very large and very bright," said the girl.

"It's too large; it makes one feel like an atom."

5   "Is not that the right way to feel—in a church?" Isabel asked, with a faint but interested smile.

"I suppose it's the right way to feel everywhere, when one *is* nobody. But I like it in a church as little as anywhere else."

10   "You ought indeed to be a Pope!" Isabel exclaimed, remembering something he had said to her in Florence.

"Ah, I should have enjoyed that!" said Gilbert Osmond.

Lord Warburton meanwhile had joined Ralph Touchett, and the two strolled away together.

15   "Who is the gentleman speaking to Miss Archer?" his lordship inquired.

"His name is Gilbert Osmond—he lives in Florence," Ralph said.

"What is he besides?"

"What's your opinion of St Peter's?" Mr Osmond was meanwhile inquiring of our young lady.

"It's very large and very bright," she contented herself with replying.

5   "It's too large; it makes one feel like an atom."

"Isn't that the right way to feel in the greatest of human temples?" she asked with rather a liking for her phrase.

"I suppose it's the right way to feel everywhere, when
10   one *is* nobody. But I like it in a church as little as anywhere else."

"You ought indeed to be a Pope!" Isabel exclaimed, remembering something he had referred to in Florence.

"Ah, I should have enjoyed that!" said Gilbert Osmond.

15   Lord Warburton meanwhile had joined Ralph Touchett, and the two strolled away together. "Who's the fellow speaking to Miss Archer?" his lordship demanded.

"His name's Gilbert Osmond—he lives in Florence," Ralph said.

20   "What is he besides?"

109

20 "Nothing at all. Oh yes, he is an American; but one forgets that; he is so little of one."

"Has he known Miss Archer long?"

"No, about a fortnight."

"Does she like him?"

25 "Yes, I think she does."

"Is he a good fellow?"

Ralph hesitated a moment. "No, he's not," he said, at last.

"Why then does she like him?" pursued Lord War-
30 burton, with noble *naiveté*.

"Because she's a woman."

Lord Warburton was silent a moment. "There are other men who *are* good fellows," he presently said, "and them—and them—"

35 "And them she likes also!" Ralph interrupted, smiling.

"Oh, if you mean she likes him in that way!" And Lord Warburton turned round again. As far as he was concerned, however, the party was broken up. Isabel remained in conversation with the gentleman from
40 Florence till they left the church, and her English lover consoled himself by lending such attention as he might to the strains which continued to proceed from the choir.

V

One of the most complex and most important series of changes occurs in the last few paragraphs of the book, where Isabel, having returned to England so that she can be with her dying cousin, is confronted by Caspar Goodwood. Her husband, Osmond, has shown himself to be a monster of callous selfishness, even to the extent of forbidding her to go on such an errand as this and Goodwood tries to persuade her to leave him.

"Nothing at all. Oh yes, he's an American, but one forgets that—he's so little of one."

"Has he known Miss Archer long?"

"Three or four weeks."

25 "Does she like him?"

"She's trying to find out."

"And will she?"

"Find out—?" Ralph asked.

"Will she like him?"

30 "Do you mean will she accept him?"

"Yes," said Lord Warburton after an instant; "I suppose that's what I horribly mean."

"Perhaps not if one does nothing to prevent it," Ralph replied.

35 His lordship stared a moment, but apprehended. "Then we must be perfectly quiet?"

"As quiet as the grave. And only on the chance!" Ralph added.

"The chance she may?"

40 "The chance she may not?"

Lord Warburton took this at first in silence, but he spoke again. "Is he awfully clever?"

"Awfully," said Ralph.

His companion thought. "And what else?"

45 "What more do you want?" Ralph groaned.

"Do you mean what more does *she*?"

Ralph took him by the arm to turn him: they had to rejoin the others. "She wants nothing that *we* can give her."

50 "Ah well, if she won't have You—!" said his lordship handsomely as they went.

Henry James

"Ah, be mine as I am yours!" she heard her companion cry. He had suddenly given up argument, and his voice seemed to come through a confusion of sound.

This however, of course, was but a subjective fact, as the metaphysicians say; the confusion, the noise of waters, and all the rest of it, were in her own head. In an instant she became aware of this. "Do me the greatest kindness of all," she said. "I beseech you to go away!"

"Ah, don't say that. Don't kill me!" he cried.

She clasped her hands; her eyes were streaming with tears.

"As you love me, as you pity me, leave me alone!"

He glared at her a moment through the dusk, and the next instant she felt his arms about her, and his lips on her own lips. His kiss was like a flash of lightning; when it was dark again she was free. She never looked about her; she only darted away from the spot. There were lights in the windows of the house; they shone far across the lawn. In an extraordinarily short time—for the distance was considerable—she had moved through the darkness (for she saw nothing) and reached the door. Here only she paused. She looked all about her; she listened a little; then she put her hand on the latch. She had not known where to turn; but she knew now. There was a very straight path.

The Portrait of a Lady

"Ah, be mine as I'm yours!" she heard her companion cry. He had suddenly given up argument, and his voice seemed to come, harsh and terrible, through a confusion of vaguer sounds.

5 This however, of course, was but a subjective fact, as the metaphysicians say; the confusion, the noise of waters, all the rest of it, were in her own swimming head. In an instant she became aware of this. "Do me the greatest kindness of all," she panted. "I beseech you to go away!"

10 "Ah, don't say that. Don't kill me!" he cried.

She clasped her hands; her eyes were streaming with tears. "As you love me, as you pity me, leave me alone!"

He glared at her a moment through the dusk, and the next instant she felt his arms about her and his lips on her

15 own lips. His kiss was like white lightning, a flash that spread, and spread again, and stayed; and it was extraordinarily as if, while she took it, she felt each thing in his hard manhood that had least pleased her, each aggressive fact of his face, his figure, his presence, justified of its

20 intense identity and made one with this act of possession. So had she heard of those wrecked and under water following a train of images before they sink. But when darkness returned she was free. She never looked about her; she only darted from the spot. There were lights in

25 the windows of the house; they shone far across the lawn. In an extraordinarily short time—for the distance was considerable—she had moved through the darkness (for she saw nothing) and reached the door. Here only she paused. She looked all about her; she listened a little;

30 then she put her hand on the latch. She had not known where to turn; but she knew now. There was a very straight path.

Two days afterwards, Caspar Goodwood knocked at the
door of the house in Wimpole Street in which Henrietta
Stackpole occupied furnished lodgings. He had hardly
removed his hand from the knocker when the door was
30   opened, and Miss Stackpole herself stood before him. She
had on her bonnet and jacket; she was on the point of
going out.

"Oh, good morning," he said, "I was in hope I should
find Mrs Osmond."

35   Henrietta kept him waiting a moment for her reply;
but there was a good deal of expression about Miss
Stackpole even when she was silent.

"Pray what led you to suppose she was here?"

"I went down to Gardencourt this morning, and the
40   servant told me she had come to London. He believed
she was to come to you."

Again Miss Stackpole held him—with an intention of
perfect kindness—in suspense.

"She came here yesterday, and spent the night. But
45   this morning she started for Rome."

Caspar Goodwood was not looking at her; his eyes were
fastened on the doorstep.

"Oh, she started—" he stammered. And without
finishing his phrase, or looking up, he turned away.

50   Henrietta had come out, closing the door behind her,
and now she put out her hand and grasped his arm.

"Look here, Mr Goodwood," she said; "just you wait!"

On which he looked up at her.

Two days afterwards Caspar Goodwood knocked at the
door of the house in Wimpole Street in which Henrietta
35   Stackpole occupied furnished lodgings. He had hardly
removed his hand from the knocker when the door was
opened and Miss Stackpole herself stood before him. She
had on her hat and jacket; she was on the point of going
out. "Oh, good morning," he said, "I was in hopes I
40   should find Mrs Osmond."

Henrietta kept him waiting a moment for her reply;
but there was a good deal of expression about Miss Stackpole even when she was silent. "Pray what led you to
suppose she was here?"

45   "I went down to Gardencourt this morning, and the
servant told me she had come to London. He believed
she was to come to you."

Again Miss Stackpole held him—with an intention of
perfect kindness—in suspense. "She came here yester-
50   day, and spent the night. But this morning she started
for Rome."

Caspar Goodwood was not looking at her; his eyes were
fastened on the doorstep. "Oh, she started—?" he
stammered. And without finishing his phrase or looking
55   up he stiffly averted himself. But he couldn't otherwise
move.

Henrietta had come out, closing the door behind her,
and now she put out her hand and grasped his arm.
"Look here, Mr Goodwood," she said; "just you wait!"

60   On which he looked up at her—but only to guess, from
her face, with a revulsion, that she simply meant he was
young. She stood shining at him with that cheap comfort,
and it added, on the spot, thirty years to his life. She
walked him away with her, however, as if she had given
65   him now the key to patience.

Virginia Woolf

'How to get over, how to escape from, the besotting *particularity* of fiction. "Roland approached the house; it had green doors and window blinds; and there was a scraper on the upper step." To hell with Roland and the scraper!'[1]

There comes a time—indeed there frequently recurs a time—when most novelists echo Stevenson's words. Virginia Woolf did so, with considerable amplification, in her essay on the modern novel in *The Common Reader*, when she wrote: '. . . let us hazard the opinion that for us at this moment the form of fiction most in vogue more often misses than secures the thing we seek. Whether we call it life or spirit, truth or reality, this, the essential thing, has moved off, or on, and refuses to be contained any longer in such ill-fitting vestments as we provide. Nevertheless, we go on perseveringly, conscientiously, constructing our two and thirty chapters after a design which more and more ceases to resemble the vision in our minds. So much of the enormous labour of proving the solidity, the likeness to life, of the story is not merely labour thrown away but labour misplaced to the extent of obscuring and blotting out the light of the conception.'[2]

[1] *The Letters of Robert Louis Stevenson*, ed. Sidney Colvin. Quoted by Robert Liddell in *Some Principles of Fiction*. Cape.
[2] Written in 1919—reprinted in *The Common Reader* (1925).

Mrs Dalloway

The reader should bear this in mind when speculating on the extracts in this section, drawn from the manuscript of *Mrs Dalloway*, for it was in that novel—some would call it her best—that Virginia Woolf was finally to shake off those stiff 'ill-fitting vestments'.

It was written in three large note-books, in ink (apart from a few pencilled memoranda) on one side only of the plain leaves, down each of which had been ruled in blue pencil a thick line, giving a margin some two inches wide. When I examined it, the manuscript had only recently been acquired by the British Museum and the note-books still had their limp and rather tattered cloth backs. (Add. MSS. 51,044–46.)

At first the general impression is one of great disorder. Turning one of the much and seemingly sketchily altered pages of the novel, the reader is as likely to come upon a rewritten and equally heavily altered version of the same passage, or an essay destined for *The Common Reader*, or a book review, as that page's logical continuation. On closer examination, however, as with Blake, one detects a keenly methodical mind at work behind the apparent disorder. It is methodical, for instance, even highly professionally methodical, to allot certain parts of one's day to very different forms of literary activity, as she did, whether one chooses to use the same note-book for both or not. And although the impression given by some of the alterations is one of sketchiness, almost of indiscriminately impatient sketchiness, it is soon found to be wrong. Virginia Woolf, it becomes clear, used the manuscript page as a painter uses a palette—quickly laying down words and phrases, images and observations, and as quickly altering them: diluting or thickening them, obliterating some and sparing others, with little regard for their syntactic settings. That—the tidying, the neatly fitting in—could be attended to later, probably during the typing. Thus 'first things first' seems to have been the over-riding consideration, and it is difficult to think of a method more ruthlessly logical, less sketchily haphazard, than that. But to recapture something of the very spirit of this one should try to reconstitute in longhand the more heavily altered of the following passages. Of all the examples in the present study, when subjected to this most useful procedure, these communicate the most vividly the feel—the very rhythm and pace—of the original writing.

Since they all concern the same thing—the book's opening passage—they should be considered as a group. I have therefore lettered rather than numbered them.

A

This is the original opening, from the first manuscript page, dated June 27, 1923, and headed 'The Hours'. It contains comparatively few alterations and one should ask oneself why.

In Westminster, whose temples, meeting houses, conventicles, and steeples of all kinds are congregated together, there is, at all hours and half hours, a sound of bells, ~~supplementing~~ correcting each other, asseverating
5   that time has come a little earlier, or stayed a little later, here or here. Thus when Mr Walsh walking with his head ~~a little~~ down, and his coat flying loose came out by the Abbey the clock of St Margarets was saying two minutes later than Big Ben that it was half past eleven. But her
10   voice was a womans voice, since it is impossible to have anything to do with inanimate objects without giving them sex, and [1] the very stair rods have character, and should fate send them to the old furniture shop and their owners pass by their voices would be heard in their own
15   accents bringing back countless passages up and down stairs, moments —[2] of happiness, or despair, moments

[1] Placed above the comma, seemingly tentatively.
[2] Deleted short word, hard to distinguish—looks like 'too'.

not otherwise communicable, for there has attached itself
even to the stair rod, something that lies below words.
~~St Margaret~~'s[1] spoke as a woman speaks, ~~with~~ there was a
20 vibration in the core of the sound, so that each word, or
note, comes fluttering, alive, yet with some reluctantce to
inflict its vitality, some grief for the past which holds it
back, some impulse nevertheless to glide into the recesses
of the heart and there bury itself in ring after ring of
25 sound, so that Mr Walsh, as he walked past St Margaret's,
and heard the bells toll the half hour felt . . .[2] only all that
surrounded it, only its futility. For he had never married
her, he had failed. But he now loved more passionately
than then, this girl in India . . .[3] He had been sent down
30 from Oxford. He had drunk too much. He had been a
socialist. But the future of ~~the Hu~~[4] civilisation lies, ~~he~~
in the hands of such young men. Of such young men as
himself, he meant.

B

The first passage ends there. On the next page the author
begins again.

    He heard Clarissa say "My party tonight" as he shut the
door. Her voice was ~~taken~~[5] ~~up~~ overwhelmed by the roar
of ~~the~~ Westminster. It became instantly refined and
spiritual, ~~like~~ and very far away, and ~~yet~~ it went on
5 echoing in his head, as he walked, as he passed a ~~very~~
man in a tail coat wearing a buttonhole, ~~as he~~ a very
smartly dressed man, a despicable specimen, thought
Peter, ~~a~~ It must be Ascot, he thought; and he became

[1] No alternative given.
[2,3] V. W.'s own punctuation.
[4] Probably the beginning of 'Human Race'.
[5] Probably 'taken', though it is difficult to read this word.

aware of all the towers which rise above the little streets,
10   the Abbey, the Houses of Parliament, Westminster Hall.
[¹There they sit, he thought, thinking of the Government,
of ~~Institutions, of settled ways~~. ~~Mantling nonsense,~~
~~he thought, and~~] "Remember my party tonight"
"remember my party he went on saying to himself. She's
15   grown worldly—She's hard, he thought to himself,
~~becoming more and more annoyed~~ Here is my Elizabeth!
he repeated. Elizabeth didn't like that. ~~She always was a~~
~~little sentimental~~ Remember my party, he repeated,
~~until~~, sarcastically, until, outside ~~We²~~ St Margarets,
20   suddenly the clock tolled the half hour and as each note
came fluttering down, alive, yet with some reluctance to
inflict its vitality, some grief for the past which held it
back, some impulse nevertheless to glide into the heart
and there bury itself in ring after ring of sound Clarissa
25   herself seemed ~~to be~~ with him. She has been ill, he thought,
and the sound expressed languor and suffering. It was her
heart, he ~~thought~~ remembered, and the bell tolled for
death that surprised in the midst of life. Mournfully

C

The second attempted opening ends there, three-quarters of
the way down the page. On the next page we find this:

He ~~heard Clarissa~~ say "~~My party tonight~~" as he shut the
~~door~~, and her voice, overwhelmed by the roar of Westminster, and the sounds of all the clocks, became
~~instantly~~ refined—spiritual and very far away, as ~~Mr~~
5   Peter Walsh shut the door.

---

¹ For the sake of clarity I have placed square brackets round lines
deleted by quick diagonal strokes of the pen.
² Probably beginning of 'Westminster'.

D

After this third attempt, the rest of the page is left blank. On the next page there is the fourth attempt, which was to hold good until the whole of the first draft of the book was completed.

It might have been the seat of time itself, this island of Westminster, the forge where the hours were made, and sent out, in various tones and tempers, to —[1] glide into the lives of the foot passengers, of studious workers, ~~of the~~
5 desultory women,[2] who coming to the window, looked up at the sky as the clock struck, as if to ~~ask~~ ask say, ~~Yes?~~ ~~Well?~~ What? ~~What next?~~ or Why? ~~To which questions~~ ~~of studious workers, of~~ to which questions ~~there~~ And ~~t~~They had their choice of answers; ~~they could select~~ from
10 the different sounds ~~they could now colliding or~~ colliding, or running side by side, melting into each other, forming ~~a~~ , for the moment, a trellis work of sound ~~over the roofs~~, which, as it faded away, was suddenly renewed from some other steeple; St Margarets, for example, ~~supple~~[3] saying
15 two minutes after Big Ben how now, really and indeed, it was half past eleven, ~~though in~~ Yes, it was half past eleven, St Margaret's said, in her sad voice, ~~her woman's~~ ~~voice~~, upon hearing which, ~~of course it~~ was necessary to make haste, or again to loiter; or ~~perhaps some~~ there
20 ~~might be some mistake about it~~, to attempt some kind of comparison. ~~Half past eleven~~ or to think how ~~very queer~~ ~~it was~~, not merely that ~~the~~ time ~~should differ, but that the~~ ~~voices of these clocks~~, differeds[4] but that the tone of it was possessed of the strangest power; ~~was~~ now militant

---

[1] Short indistinguishable word deleted. Possibly 'be'.
[2] Written above 'women' and deleted is a word that might have been 'womanhood'.
[3] Probably beginning of 'supplementing'.
[4] The 's' written above the undeleted 'ed'.

25 and masculine; now ~~so~~ curtly prosaic, and now in the
voice of St Margaret's ~~had the power to brush every leaf~~
~~and flower in the mind~~, and had the power, like some
breeze which visits a garden at dawn, to brush every
flower and leaf in the mind's territory, ~~to set stirring and~~
30 ~~flashing~~ lifting, stirring, strangely, very strangely.

Remember my party, remember my party, said Peter
Walsh as he stepped down the street, with the sound
~~giving~~ of Big Ben in his ears, swinging downright, direct,
~~vigorous, like the punch of a young man striking out ever~~
35 ~~so lustily this way and that, with irresistible vigour~~, and
———[1] ~~on the~~ rhythmically in time with the flow of the
sound the direct downright sound of Big Ben striking the
half hour; ~~Clarissa's parties, he thought~~ Clarissa's parties
—why does Clarissa give parties? ~~he thought~~. Not that
40 he blamed her. He blamed nobody. Only he was glad to
be himself. And he saw himself advancing in the plate
glass window of a motor car manufacturers, like a figure
which has escaped. All India lay behind him—its plains
and mountains, the epidemics he had mastered, the deci-
45 sions he had made alone, by himself, which affect~~ing~~ed the
lives of thousands; ~~while here, he thought, they~~ ~~She~~
Clarissa had grown hard, he thought, and a trifle sentimental he thought, and he stopped in front of the window,
looking at the great motor cars. He had a turn for mecha-
50 nics. He had invented a plough in his district, and ordered
wheelbarrows from England, but the coolies wouldn't use
them. The way she said, "Here is my Elizabeth!"—that
annoyed me, he thought. And Elizabeth didn't like it
either,—Still the last tremors of the great voice of the
55 clock shook the air round him, ~~and stirring~~ For he under-
stood young people, young ~~men, young women~~ ~~Clarissa~~

[1] Deleted word difficult to distinguish. Could be 'till' without cross of
't' and dot over 'i'; or 'fell' (to make 'fell on the').

~~was always cold~~, and liked them;[1] there was always something cold about <u>Clarissa</u>, he thought. She had always, ~~a~~
even when I first knew her, a <u>sort of timidity</u> ~~of mind~~
60 ~~and~~ ,which in middle age, ~~he thought, that kind of~~ becomes
conventionality. and then its all up, its all up! he thought,
looking rather drearily into the glassy depths, and wondering whether ~~somehow~~, by his appearance, or calling at that
hour, he had annoyed her? ~~Like a~~ With the same ~~effect~~
65 ~~as~~ sudden that[2] a cloud ~~has~~, on a summer day, cross~~ing~~<u>es</u>
the sun, silence falls on London; and falls on the mind,
~~and~~ all effort[3] ceases. Time flaps on the mast. Rigid,
like a skeleton, ~~only~~ the skeleton of belief <u>alone</u> upholds
the human frame. Blankness, ~~indifference~~ glances[4] from
70 pavement from plate glass windows, ~~blankness and~~
~~indifference~~. She refused me, he thought.

Ah, said St Margarets, like a hostess who comes into
her drawing room ~~and~~ <u>on</u> the very stroke of the hour and
finds her guests there already, I am not late. No, it is
75 precisely half past eleven. ~~She says like a~~[5] ~~And~~ <u>But</u> ~~her~~
~~voice~~ although she is perfectly right, her voice is somehow
reluc<u>t</u>ant to inflict its ~~vitality~~ <u>vitality</u>[6], some grief for the
past holds it back; some concern ~~a~~ ~~sensitiveness~~ ~~perhaps~~,

---

[1] In the margin at the side of the passage, with no exact indication
where it was to be inserted. In the preceding deletion the first 'young'
was obviously missed by the hasty stroke.

[2] Obviously Virginia Woolf meant 'effect' to stand and the phrase to
be 'sudden effect that'—but didn't stop to tidy up. The image of the
cloud crossing the sun was really what mattered.

[3] Could be 'affront' and indeed looks more like it—though in printed
text (p. 55—Chatto edition) where this passage was eventually used in
modified form, we have 'Effort ceases'.

[4] Possible reading of a word difficult to distinguish.

[5] Deleted in pencil—one of the very few places where this is used in the
manuscript.

[6] Virginia Woolf herself must at first have been somewhat at a loss
when re-examining this semi-deletion, for in the margin is written
'certainly individuality'.

~~for feeling~~ for the present. It is half past eleven she says,
80 ~~and~~ the sound glides into the recesses of the heart and
buries itself in ring after ring of sound, ~~fluttering~~ like
something alive which wants to confide itself, ~~to~~ to
~~dissipate~~ disperse itself, to be, with an ~~exquisite~~ tremor
of delight, at rest. ~~So Mr Walsh felt as if Clarissa, were~~
85 ~~with him[1]~~ . ~~leaving her drawing room~~, like Clarissa herself, thought Peter Walsh ~~coming out in by the~~ coming
~~along the lawn with her hands full of something to~~ after
~~him~~ me, in white, ~~alto For She came back, as a whole,~~
~~much more truly like this~~. As ~~if years ago there had~~
90 come into some room where ~~they sat together~~ This is
Clarissa he thought, with ~~an ext~~ a deep emotion, and an
extraordinarily clear yet puzzling recollection of her, as
if this bell had come into the room, years ago, where they
sat, at some moment of great intimacy, and ~~had n had kept~~
95 ~~had it in its keeping, and now~~ and had gone from one to
the other and ~~then now poured~~ and left laden with the
moment[2] But what room? and what moment? And then as
the sound withdrew ~~he thought~~ She has been ill, and the
sound expressed languor and suffering. It was her heart,
100 he remembered, and the sudden loudness of the bell
tolled for death that surprised in the midst of life, Clarissa
falling where she stood, in her drawing room. No, no!
he cried. She is not dead. I am not old. He was glaring
~~with~~ almost ferociously at the statue of the Duke of
105 Cambridge.

And he looked ~~as he~~ up Whitehall as if his future were

[1] 'were with him' deleted first; comma then added after 'Clarissa'.
[2] These words in margin. The last word is very difficult to make out.
It could be 'hour', though the printed text suggests that it was probably
a scribbled 'moment'. It is interesting to note that in the manuscript
Virginia Woolf leaves out—probably in her haste to transfer her thoughts
to paper—the bee image itself, though this is of course brought into the
printed text (p. 56).

spread before him, and ~~he had only to step out briskly towards it~~. He was not old, or set, or shrivelled, and as for caring what people said here in England, he cared not a
110 rap, he cared not a rap. So squaring himself with his cheeks all in a wrinkle, he glared at the ~~statue of the~~ statue of the Duke of Cambridge. ———[1] It was true that he was a failure. He had been sent down from Oxford. He had drunk too much. He had been a socialist. Still the future
115 of civilisation lies, he thought, in the hands of such young men. Of such young men as himself, he ~~thought~~, meant, with their courage, their loneliness, their passion for scientific truth,[2] thinking, as no one else ~~can~~ could possibly think, of how ~~right~~ he had been, and[3] right and
120 truly courageous, and ~~how, though a~~ outwardly ~~unstable~~, he had always kept up his faith in science ~~and~~ and in knowledge and read in mathematics.

E

On October 9, 1924, Virginia Woolf completed the first draft of her novel. It had taken nearly twenty-eight months to reach this point and during this time the title had been changed to *Mrs Dalloway*. (There is an interesting entry in the manuscript on one of the blank pages opposite the drafted Elizabeth/ Miss Kilman tea-time passages—i.e., about three-quarters of the way through the book—where various titles are tried out: The life of a Lady; A lady; Mrs Dalloway (all in ink, deleted) and A ladies portrait; A lady of Fashion (both in pencil, undeleted).) On October 20, 1924, she started to rewrite the

[1] Indistinguishable word deleted.
[2] These words in margin, with no precise indication of where they were to be inserted.
[3] Comma and 'and' left undeleted.

opening yet again, temporarily reverting to the title *The Hours*, with which she headed it.

Mrs Dalloway said she would buy the flowers herself. For Lucy had her work cut ~~ef~~ out for her. The doors would be taken off their hinges; Rumpelmayers men were coming. And then, thought Clarissa, what a day!

5 What ~~an ecstasy~~! a ~~miracle~~! ~~ecstasy~~![1] lark! What a plunge! For so it had always seemed to her, when, with a little squeak of the hinges which she could hear now, she had burst open the French windows ~~as~~ and ~~stepped out on to the terrace at Bourton~~, and plunged at Bourton 10 ~~into the terrace~~ into the open air. ~~Like waves, like~~ How fresh, how calm, stiller than this of course, ~~and~~ the air was in the early morning; rooks cawing, dogs barking; ~~and the~~ ——[2], ~~which naturally one lost later~~ ——[3] ~~and then, rooks cawing, dogs barking; and and with it all~~ 15 ~~—but Peter Walsh she~~[4] ~~would say she~~ like the flap of a wave; like the kiss of ~~a~~ wave; ~~for~~—chill and sharp and yet, (for a girl of eighteen as she was then) ~~how~~ . ~~and a~~[5] ~~little~~ solemn, ~~yes, solemn~~. Peter Walsh would say— whatever Peter Walsh did say— ~~when he found when he~~ 20 ~~found her~~ "Musing among the vegetables?" Wasn't that it? Peter who didn't know a rose from a cauliflower, and "preferred men to cabbages." She "I prefer men to cabbages." He must have said it at breakfast, for her to be thinking of it on the terrace, in a morning, ~~and then~~ 25 ~~going~~[6] ~~she had out on to the terrace~~, and she had gone

---

[1] 'ecstasy!' was reinstated, presumably after the deletion of 'miracle!' by putting a printer's *stet* line under the word.

[2] Indistinguishable word deleted—looks rather like 'terrace'.

[3] Indistinguishable word deleted.

[4] 'she' deleted before the rest.

[5] 'and' (written as an ampersand) and 'a' combined, the latter apparently written on top of the former before deletion of both.

[6] 'going' deleted before the rest.

on to the terrace, as she had done over and over again,
~~with to escape, to look, to think it over, what Peter said
and how the morning looked~~ and stood there, just for a
moment, and felt as she could not feel now, ~~at her age,~~
30 that something tremendous was about to happen, but
~~that~~ and so stood, and so looked, at the flowers, at the
trees, and wondered why, then, ~~that~~ this young man,
whom they hardly knew, should begin like that, to Aunt
Helena of all people, at breakfast. ~~Not to like flowers~~!
35 It was very like him. And he would be back from India
one of these days, June or July, she forgot which, ~~and
to be perfectly honest~~ she had ~~for she never could not read~~
his letters; they were awfully dry; it was his sayings one
remembered, his big pocket knife, his eyes; his ~~charm too~~;
40 and his grumpiness; and ~~when~~[1] millions of things ~~were~~
had utterly vanished, a few ~~sayin~~things. like this. ~~which
brought back to her that~~ about cabbages.

The most profitable line of study here would seem to be as
follows:

1. Follow the progression from A to D, noting particularly the
change in style and the crystallization of certain images and
ideas.

2. Compare D with the final version, as printed on pp. 54–57
of the Hogarth Press edition.

3. Speculate on the probable reasons for using the passage at
this point of the novel instead of at the beginning, as originally
intended.

4. Examine D for what might have been germinating ideas
for the new beginning, E.

5. Compare E itself with the published text (p. 5 of the
Hogarth Press edition).

[1] The deletion here is of the wild, scrawled variety, barely touching the
word, and might well have indicated a more general dissatisfaction with
that part of the passage.